# ROOTED IN FAITH

MEDITATIONS FROM THE REFORMERS

COMPILED AND EDITED BY
BERNARD BANGLEY

PARACLETE PRESS
Brewster, Massachusetts

Unless otherwise designated, Scripture quotations are taken from the Holy Bible, New International Version. Copyright 1973, 1978, 1984 International Bible Society. Used by permission of Zondervan Publishers.

Scripture quotations designated (NRSV) are from the Revised Standard Version of the Bible, copyright 1989 by the Division of Christian Education of the National Council of the Churches of Christ in the USA. All rights reserved. Used by permission.

Scripture quotations designated KJV are from the King James Version of the Bible.

Library of Congress Cataloging-in-Publication Data
Rooted in faith : meditations from the reformers / compiled and edited by Bernard Bangley
    p. cm.
  ISBN 1-55725-345-5
1. Devotional calendars. 2. Protestant churches—Doctrines—Meditations. I. Bangley, Bernard, 1935–
  BV4810.R66 2003
  242' .2—dc22
                                                    2003015219

10 9 8 7 6 5 4 3 2 1

© 2003 by Bernard Bangley

ISBN: 1-55725-345-5

All rights reserved. No portion of this book may be reproduced, stored in an electronic retrieval system, or transmitted in any form or by any means—electronic, mechanical, photocopy, recording, or any other—except for brief quotations in printed reviews, without the prior permission of the publisher.

Published by Paraclete Press
Brewster, Massachusetts
www.paracletepress.com
Printed in the United States of America.

# CONTENTS

Introduction

JANUARY: *Spiritual Seeking*
1

FEBRUARY: *Attentiveness to the Spirit*
25

MARCH: *With God in Difficult Times*
45

APRIL: *Mystery of God*
67

MAY: *Christian Relationships*
87

JUNE: *Faith*
111

JULY: *Patience and Contentment*
131

AUGUST: *Prayer*
155

SEPTEMBER: *Inner Life*
177

OCTOBER: *Scripture*
199

NOVEMBER: *Life in Christ*
221

DECEMBER: *Signs and Symbols of Christian Life*
243

BIOGRAPHICAL INFORMATION
265

# INTRODUCTION

WHO IS A PROTESTANT? I know a person with no church affiliation at all who stated on a questionnaire that he was a Protestant because he was not a Catholic. Many today can define Protestantism only in terms of what it is not. This negative slant is exacerbated by the obvious use of "protest" as its base word. To protest today is to disapprove and object; it is a complaint. Protest marches for TV cameras have become a familiar part of life. While there can be no doubt that the early reformers had plenty to complain about, the deeper understanding of "protest" is to make a solemn declaration—an affirmation of principle.

Many pages of early Protestant writing devote much ink to opposing the "Papists" and establishing a doctrinal basis for position, and frankly, such material is not very uplifting to read today. Few complete books on devotion and spirituality are available from that era, because the writers were simply too busy carving out a place to stand.

But a treasure trove of spiritual and devotional guidance is mingled with the polemic. Martin Luther's *Table Talk* opens a window on unguarded comments among friends that stands far apart from his heavier writing. The spiritual passion of Jonathan Edwards breaks out like a sunbeam in a stormy sky; and the simple faith of Anne Hutchinson is as calming as the Book of Ruth, sandwiched in the Old Testament among all those grim accounts of war and conquest. Finding these wonderful expressions of glowing spirituality is not exactly like searching for a needle in a haystack, but it takes a lot of reading to discover each gem. The design of this book is a perfect forum for these scattered flashes of spiritual insight from early Protestant writers.

Women authors were present in the era, but not in the spotlight. Because women of the time were taught little other than to read and write, most women writers had to educate themselves. Most of their work exists today only in their diaries, correspondence, tracts, and poetry. This collection includes inspiring passages from many of these more obscure female authors. Their warmly human personal writings offer a welcome and naturally contrasting quality.

During the years prior to the Reformation the Christian Church had honestly attempted to cleanse itself. Martin Luther did not act without long historic preparation; many others had recognized and denounced the human shortcomings of the Church. We may think of critics such as John Wycliffe, William Tyndale, Girolamo Savonarola, and John Huss as pre-reformers. They were not formally separated from the Church, but their ideas set them apart. Some were martyred.

Both Catholics and Protestants have bloodied the history of Christianity with ruthless persecution of people who have held minority views. "Heresy" has not often been tolerated. Being "orthodox" means to think correctly. Many leaders across the centuries have urged toleration, but few have heeded. The logical conclusion seemed to many that if salvation depended upon a proper faith, then heretics were leading people astray and toleration was impossible. Early Protestants expressed their ideas at great risk to life and limb. Montaigne commented, "It is setting a high value on one's opinions to roast men on account of them."

Resentment in Europe built to a fever pitch through the Middle Ages. In the seventeenth century the walls of tradition and reverence came tumbling down. A religious upheaval swept across the Continent and the British Isles, which was was more significant and life-changing than all the political revolutions of recent years. A radical transfer of wealth and authority accompanied alterations in church doctrine. Important Protestant teaching introduced the priesthood of all believers and the supreme authority of the Scriptures. An emphasis on preaching pushed the sacraments into a secondary role.

The Protestant Reformation developed in unique ways in England and America. Henry VIII severed British ties with the Pope and assumed leadership of the Church of England. He continued to support Catholic dogma and had little regard for Martin Luther. Aside from the action of the king, no single individual stands out as the driving force behind the development of reformed thinking in England. During the turmoil of religious reformation in Europe, large numbers of immigrants from various cultures came to America. Instead of settling in established communities with traditional values, they pioneered in an ever-changing wilderness. Their descendants adapted their religious inheritance from an advancing frontier to an industrialized and urbanized nation. The "Great Awakening," inspired by Jonathan Edwards, began an era of revivalism that had far-reaching effects on the nation's religious orientation. These changes continue in the present time, with so-called "mainline" Protestant denominations coping with the rise of popular independent churches that understand the use of electronics in an entertainment-centered culture. As might be expected in a religion that developed in a frontier atmosphere, American Protestantism has always stressed individual piety.

I have chosen selections from the widest possible collection of authors. Represented here are Anabaptists, Anglicans, Episcopalians, Lutherans, Methodists, Presbyterians, Quakers, Puritans, Unitarians, and others. They do not always agree with each other. Contradictory positions give a conversational tone to the compilation.

Every entry has been modernized. In a few cases, all that was needed was to replace an obsolete word with its nearest modern equivalent. Most selections have been thoroughly paraphrased in crisp, clear English for easy reading. The ideas and illustrations remain as in the original. Unless noted otherwise, all

# INTRODUCTION

Scripture quotations are from the New International Version.

The selections are arranged in twelve broad categories, one for each month of the year, with a specific reading dated for each day of the year. If this daily approach appeals to you, this organization will make it easy to keep up. Of course, you may find great interest in reading from these selections at random.

# JANUARY
## *Spiritual Seeking*

JANUARY 1

## *Divine Instruction*

Most worthwhile things take effort to learn. Being a sinner is easy, but religion requires careful instruction. Spiritual lessons often contradict nature. Self-denial, saving all by losing all, becoming fools that we might be wise—such things do not make sense until our own will has melted into God's will. It is necessary to learn how to be dead to the world and how to have plenty when you have little. Religion is not always golden and crowned with jewels. Sometimes we must follow Christ down a dark path when faith is dressed in its night-clothes.

This is an unnatural thing to do. We must throw a stone violently if it is to ascend into the air. There is violence in the soul's movement toward heaven; it requires training. Beg the Spirit of God to teach you. We have need of divine instruction. Unless sunlight falls on a sundial it is pointless to study it. We may read the Bible repeatedly, but we will not discover the point of it all until the Spirit teaches us. "For God, who said, 'Let light shine out of darkness,' made his light shine in our hearts to give us the light of the knowledge of the glory of God in the face of Christ" (2 Corinthians 4:6). Others may tell us our lesson, but only God can teach us. Two people may listen to the same sermon and respond quite differently.

—Thomas Watson: *The Art of Divine Contentment*

JANUARY 2

## The Joy of Meditation

Frequently read the works of Christian writers. Attend church and pay full attention to sermons. Such things are of the utmost importance if you want to make progress in the spiritual life.

Your thoughts about, and feelings toward, a family member are strong. Possibly not a day passes when you do not think of a loved one. There are pleasing thoughts regarding your time together.

You are infinitely more obligated to Christ than to any family member. Think about him. Meditate upon his sufferings. Imagine him upon the cross, dying for you. Turn your thoughts to heaven where he still lives and intercedes for you. Consider this best of all beings looking down on you with an eye of inexpressible benevolence. He speaks to you the most encouraging words imaginable: "Come to me, all you who are weary and burdened, and I will give you rest" (Matthew 11:28).

It is not sufficient to think of these things now and then, at distant intervals. The more often you think of them, the more pleasure you will take in such meditations. The more you think of Christ, the more you will *want* to think of Christ.

—Hannah Sinclair: *A Letter to Catherine*

JANUARY 3

## Growth

As a Christian grows, there is an increase in mellowness. Poison ivy grows as fast as a rose, but the rose becomes sweet. A crabapple develops alongside a pear, but one has a harsh, sour taste, while the other becomes delicious. A hypocrite may grow outwardly as much as a true Christian. There will be plenty of prayer and testimony, but the hypocrite's growth is only in size. Pride leavens duties. The believer ripens as he grows. He grows in love, humility, and faith.

A Christian grows in strength, becoming rooted and firmly established. The more a tree grows, the more it spreads its roots in the earth. As a plant in God's vineyard, a Christian grows more deeply into Christ, drawing spiritual sap from him. "Your faith is growing more and more, and the love every one of you has for each other is increasing" (2 Thessalonians 1:3).

—Thomas Watson: *The Art of Divine Contentment*

JANUARY 4

## The Way to God

There is no need to soar above the clouds or to travel all over the earth. We do not need to go beyond the seas or to seek God in a bottomless pit. We have his Word. God opens the door of paradise for us when we open sacred Scripture. It is almost as though he reaches out his hand visibly to receive us as his children.

How do we become one with our Lord Jesus Christ? By being pilgrims in this world and passing through it as someone who is authentically devout. St. Paul says, "You are no longer foreigners and aliens, but fellow citizens with God's people and members of God's household" (Ephesians 2:19).

—John Calvin: *Behavior in the Church*

JANUARY 5

## God Expects Prayer

God wants us to ask for help. He desires that we call upon him in difficult times. It is our responsibility to seek his assistance. In the same way that we look for water when we are thirsty, we look for God when we need strength beyond our own. "Come unto me, all you who are weary and burdened, and I will give you rest" (Matthew 11:28). God desires that we ask.

—John Hooper: *Exposition on the Sixty-second Psalm*

JANUARY 6

## It Can Be Done

Because the primary truths of religion are transcendent and only mystically apprehended, it is impossible to grip them in a logical vise. Still, thoughtful people should not give up, nor be content with a vague religiosity. There are facts that are outside of our consciousness, and above it, that will fit into facts we already know. To understand them, we have to make them our own. This is not an easy work. It is a task for the reflective side of the religious life.

—John Shairp: *Hindrances to Spiritual Growth*

JANUARY 7

## *Becoming Fruitful*

Paul prayed that we "may be pure and blameless until the day of Christ, filled with the fruit of righteousness that comes through Jesus Christ" (Philippians 1:10–11). He compares us with a grapevine, an emblem of fruitfulness. And we are encouraged to bear full clusters.

We are never too old to bear fruit. "The righteous will flourish like a palm tree, they will grow like a cedar of Lebanon; planted in the house of the LORD, they will flourish in the courts of our God. They will still bear fruit in old age, they will stay fresh and green" (Psalm 92:12–14).

Spiritual growth is continuous. We are never satisfied that we have developed enough. Renewal is a constant need. Don't be satisfied with the first sprout of grace. Grace in its infancy and youth is not enough. Be Christian by increasing degrees.

—Thomas Watson: *The Art of Divine Contentment*

JANUARY 8

## Grey Areas

Thoughtful people want to systematize knowledge. They want a completely rounded theory of the universe that includes all known facts, each assigned to its proper place. This is the root of science and philosophy. It seems like a great gain to devise a comprehensive, all-embracing map of knowledge with every object falling into its proper place. All uncertainty and cloudy horizons are rigorously shut out.

Many think this comes at a price too high. The ragged rims of knowledge are cut away. The borderland between the definitely conceived and the dimly perceived is excluded. These are the very regions where the great challenges of thought are alive.

Though the systematizers exclude such uncertainties from their system, they cannot exclude them from reality. Shut them out as you may, they will reappear, emerging from human history and consciousness.

—John Shairp: *Hindrances to Spiritual Growth*


JANUARY 9

## Psalm 63

O God, you are both God and good to me
To find you I therefore will
Employ my skill
When first my sight the morning light shall see

Within my soul a thirst of you does dwell
My body does more crave
Your taste to have
Than in this desert dry a springing well

This desert whence when I my thoughts do rear
I no less behold your might
And glory bright
Than if I in your sanctuary were...
—Mary Sidney: *The Sidney Psalter*

JANUARY 10

## Total Change

Without Christ we are totally alienated from God. We are naturally inclined to prefer almost anything above God. In this state, prayer is an irksome duty and Sundays are a wearisome bother. Church is a bore. Religious books have little appeal. Not only is any devotional exercise repugnant, there is a spirit of rebellion against God. God's commandments mean little. The most powerful motivators are self-interest, pleasure, and vanity. Any attention to God is the result of fear. There is no loving desire to please God.

St. Paul expressly says, "If anyone is in Christ, he is a new creation; the old has gone, the new has come!" (2 Corinthians 5:17). The change is dramatic. It involves the total self. Delight replaces apathy.

Christ becomes one's greatest desire. Such a changed person seeks a more intimate acquaintance and union with him.

—Hannah Sinclair: *A Letter to Catherine*

JANUARY 11

## *Educating the Soul*

We must learn some spiritual lessons. The well-educated scholar who has profound understanding of the arts and sciences had to begin simply. The ability to read begins with learning the alphabet. Being able to count requires knowing numbers. Gradually, one advances in reading and in the complexity of mathematics. Learning comes in stages, one step after another.

A Christian is a spiritual student. Christ has many lessons to teach. The soul is in Christ's school. Some of his lessons are hard. Self-denial, for instance. As a child begins a new subject there is often the complaint that the lessons are too difficult. Bradford the Martyr said, "Whoever has not learned the lesson of the cross, has not earned his ABC in Christianity." The cross is where Christ begins with his elementary students. If you mean to be a Christian you must become familiar with what Christ means when he says, "If anyone would come after me, he must deny himself and take up his cross daily and follow me" (Luke 9:23).

—Jeremiah Burroughs
*Rare Jewel of Christian Contentment*

JANUARY 12

## Respect for God

When you read the Bible, begin with genuine respect for God. Have a firm desire to reform your life according to its teaching. Pay attention and learn all you can. Later, you will be able to teach. You will not be teaching then with your mouth, but with your holy living and good example.

—Thomas Cranmer: *Prologue to the Bible*

JANUARY 13

## Empty Calories

Everything in this world is empty. "'Meaningless! Meaningless!' says the Teacher. 'Utterly meaningless! Everything is meaningless'" (Ecclesiastes 1:2). Such hollowness really is powerless to help or to hurt us. It is all but as the wind. There is nothing in this world that can feed the hungry soul. Don't think you would be happy if only you could obtain more of what the world has to offer.

The explanation for the dissatisfaction of your soul is that material things are not its food. The soul is capable of God. Many have thought they were troubled because they did not have enough possessions. If only they could obtain a little more, they would be satisfied. Suppose someone is hungry. Do you think that person could satisfy the stomach's craving by gaping wide his mouth and feasting on the wind? Would he then conclude that the reason he is not satisfied is because he has not got enough of the wind? Of course not. Wind is not a proper food for a ravenous appetite. There is the same madness in the idea that the things of the world will satisfy the needs of the soul. "Why spend money on what is not bread, and your labor on what does not satisfy?" (Isaiah 55:2).

—Jeremiah Burroughs
*Rare Jewel of Christian Contentment*

JANUARY 14

## Spiritual Turning

Don't let confidence in the Lord's mercy lead you to heap sins upon sins. If you are young, don't say, "I'll do what I want, and when I am old I will ask God to forgive me."

*Lord Jesus, completely turn us to you now. Heal us and make us whole. Without your help there is no way we can turn and be restored. Make it a permanent change. Don't let us turn to you today and turn away tomorrow.*

What is turning to God? It is turning away from a sinful world. What is turning away from God? It is giving first importance to the changeable goods of this world. A devout Christian does not care to seek any of the things the world loves.

—John Wycliffe: *The Poor Caitiff*

JANUARY 15

## *In the Beginning*

Religion began when God called runaways back to himself. Otherwise, we would have deserted God forever. Adam and Eve noticed their nakedness, their guilt. A merciful God took pity. He was like a devoted father who hates the foolishness and irresponsibility of his son, and yet cannot hate the son. He calls gently to one in desolation and despair. "Where are you?" (Genesis 3:9).

The Heavenly Father is unspeakably gracious. God, who places all things where they are (or they would be nowhere), asks Adam where he is. Moreover, he asks this question in order to help the unhappy man, showing him clearly the depth of his disobedience. Guilty Adam thought he had lost his home and hearth. He remembered God's warning: "You must not eat from the tree of the knowledge of good and evil, for when you eat of it you will surely die" (Genesis 2:17).

Here is the cradle of religion, the beginning of loyal devotion. The obstinate and wayward child runs away in despair. A loving parent makes every effort to return that child to its home. Pious devotion is complete only when we turn to the one who calls us away from ourselves and our schemes.

—Ulrich Zwingli: *On True and False Religion*

JANUARY 16

## *Trust Yourself*

We are to follow religious guides voluntarily. It is a matter of choice. Our salvation does not depend upon the thinking of another Christian. Sometimes it is the shepherd's fault that a sheep will perish. God has given us guides we are to trust, but we are also to trust our own good judgment. It is best to follow our guides if we don't see a better way, but it is always a better thing to follow a pillar of fire than a pillar of smoke, though both may possibly lead to Canaan [Exodus 13:21].

Even our acts of understanding are acts of choice. Our duty is to search the Scriptures, to test the spirits to see if they are of God, and judge for ourselves what is right. Evaluate everything and keep what is best.

—Jeremy Taylor: *The Liberty of Prophesying*

JANUARY 17

## *Another Destination*

If a traveler passes through pleasant places, flowery meadows, or shady groves, he does not stop for more than a brief time. He only takes a transient view of them as he goes along. They do not entice him enough to make him put off the thought of proceeding to his destination. The journey's end is in mind. If he discovers comfortable accommodations at an inn, he gives no thought to settling there. He understands that these things are not his own. He is but a stranger in that place. When he has been refreshed, he wants to go on with his trip, and he is pleased to think how much of the journey is now behind.

In the same way, we desire heaven more than the comforts and enjoyments of this life. Let's be above the things of this world and cheerfully part with them whenever God calls. God lends us these things for a little while, to serve the present moment. We should set our hearts on heaven as our inheritance forever. "Our salvation is nearer now than when we first believed" (Romans 13:11).

—Jonathan Edwards: *Works*

JANUARY 18

## Collision of Mind and Spirit

I have heard of devout and self-denying parents, working late and early, and stinting themselves to send their children to college. They hope that their child will return filled with knowledge and wisdom and help them with their religious questions. Sometimes the very opposite occurs. A college student returns home full of the newest ideas, but without the early piety and familiar reverence. The child has chosen a road quite different from the one they traveled.

This common tale is no less pathetic for its frequency. It illustrates the collision of a newly awakened intellect with early faith. Pain also accompanies the birth of thought.

—John Shairp: *Hindrances to Spiritual Growth*

JANUARY 19

## *Spiritual Pride*

Maintain the strictest watch against spiritual pride. You may have moments that lift up your soul with extraordinary experiences and comforts. These are the high favors of heaven that many receive. Following such a time, we need to keep an extremely careful watch on our own attitudes. We must not think of ourselves as having become eminent saints and God's special favorites, or that we have an edge on the secrets of the Lord.

Some true Christians make the mistake of paying too much attention to the strong impressions of their minds. These are not direct communications from God.

—Jonathan Edwards
*Marks of a Work of the True Spirit*


JANUARY 20

## *Religious Enthusiasts*

We might properly call Old Testament prophets and New Testament apostles "enthusiasts." The word means "inspiration from God." They were under a divine influence. "For prophecy never had its origin in the will of man, but men spoke from God as they were carried along by the Holy Spirit" (2 Peter 1:21).

The word also covers the unfortunate phenomenon of *imaginary* rather than *real* inspiration. A religious enthusiast may be a conceited person who thinks he is a person favored with the extraordinary presence of the deity. He mistakes the workings of his own passions for divine communications. He fancies himself directly inspired by the Spirit of God. All the while, he is under no other influence than that of an over-heated imagination.

—Charles Chauncy
*Enthusiasm Described and Cautioned Against*

JANUARY 21

## Differences of Opinion

A truth that is obvious to one person may be unintelligible to another. What you think is a mere rite of religion, your neighbor may hold as a fundamental principle of the gospel. No one should accept the opinion of someone else without carefully evaluating it. Speculative differences, when accompanied with Christian virtues in living, are a poor reason for fighting with other disciples who have the same Master.

—Aaron Bancroft: *Sermons*

JANUARY 22

## The Source

Always return to Christ. He is the only fountain of this spiritual life. If we cannot find it in ourselves, we will always find it in him. It steadily pours fresh from him to us. As soon as we become conscious of the void, then the risen one appears to our spirit and breathes on us his life-giving power. Drawn only from him, his heavenly gifts become more and more an inexhaustible, continually flowing fountain of spiritual and eternal life.

—Friedrich Schleiermacher: *Selected Sermons*

JANUARY 23

## Our True Home

This world is not our abiding place; our life here is brief. Our days on earth are like a shadow. God never intended that this world would be our permanent home. These are temporary accommodations. Never settle down, no matter how pleasant the circumstances around you. Enjoy them for now, work hard at your job, and take care of your family. But keep your primary thoughts on where you are going rather than on the delights around you.

—Jonathan Edwards: *Works*

JANUARY 24

## Love's Hunger

Love is necessarily miserable. It is troubled and restless because it cannot find enough that is excellent to fill the vastness of its capacity. Such an eager passion is naturally going to stir the spirit, because it can't find enough to satisfy its cravings. Because love is so large

and unlimited, it is extremely pinched and constrained when confined to earthly things. Nothing less than an infinite good can give it room to stretch itself. A little skin-deep beauty, or some small token of goodness, is not enough to satisfy a passion that was made for God. Our spirits are designed to embrace an infinite God.
 —Henry Scougal: *The Life of God in the Soul of Man*

JANUARY 25

## An Imperfect Church

When you see disorder in the Church of God, do not despair. Our Lord Jesus Christ is able to continue working in it and through it. Its beauty may be marred. It may be polluted and defiled. Still, God will be glorified. Those who trouble the church will not continue forever.

When we see that the Church is not as perfect as it ought to be, we often think that all is lost, that God is not in control. Be patient. After we have done everything we can without seeing any results, God will use the evil for good purposes.
 —John Calvin: *Vessels Unto Honor*

JANUARY 26

## Soul Struggle

Let no one be proud of having doubts and questions about religious subjects. This does not prove you are an intellectual athlete, nor does it entitle you to look down on anyone who is free from your struggle. There is a higher state, a purer atmosphere that is breathed by people as smart as you are. They have a finer spirit.

Many reach the reasoning age only to find themselves in mental blind alleys. They hesitate to tell their sad secrets to others. They shut them up within themselves and brood over them until they are magnified beyond all proportion to their reality.

What advice may we give them? Don't make little questions of great consequence, and don't make important questions of little consequence. While doubts are painful, they are not necessarily wrong. Natural honesty leads to the birth pains of larger knowledge. These are the straits through which we pass to clearer light. The only sinful doubts are the ones that come from irreverence and self-conceit.

—John Shairp: *Hindrances to Spiritual Growth*

JANUARY 27

## *Prayer of a Seeker*

O God, permeate my heart with your heavenly light and love. Let me know and love you above all things. Let me be so ravished in your wonder and love that I may forget myself and all things. Let nothing pull me away from you. Your perfection infinitely exceeds all thought and understanding. Let me find you more inwardly present with me than I am with myself. Let me be conscious that I am living in your presence, my holy Lord.

—Robert Leighton
*Rules and Instructions for a Holy Life*

JANUARY 28

## *Actions Better than Words*

Actions express the power and life of religion better than words. Actions are more vivid than spoken words. They clearly demonstrate the motivating inward principle of a devout life.

—Henry Scougal
*The Life of God in the Soul of Man*

JANUARY 29

## *The Light*

Dear Brothers and Sisters who gather in the light of Christ Jesus, the fountain of all light and life. The saints live in the light. This light leads them to its source. Here is unity of spirit and an unbreakable peace. Here the pure language of worship of the Lord is harmonious. This is a way of holiness where the unclean may not travel. The presence of the Lord is here. There is fullness of joy. This is the light of the knowledge of the glory of God that is in the face of his son Jesus Christ.

—Margaret Fell Fox: *An Epistle to Friends, 1657*

JANUARY 30

## Stopping Short

Even a secular person can find the beauty of heaven attractive. The descriptions of its glorious crowns and rivers of pleasure are enough to make anyone wish to be there. Though there be no understanding of the spiritual pleasures such metaphors and similitudes attempt to describe, a person can believe that Christ has purchased these wonderful things for him. He may feel tenderness and affection for Christ's kindness, imagining that he has much love for his Lord. All the while such an individual may remain a total stranger to the spirit of Jesus.

—Henry Scougal:*The Life of God in the Soul of Man*


JANUARY 31

## Limits of Spiritual Knowledge

We travel as far as possible into the spiritual life with the guides available to us. Beyond this, we can only use our imaginations. We say heaven is inhabited with angels and archangels, with cherubim and seraphim. We can look no farther into it with these eyes.

The Holy Spirit accommodates our limited vision. We are told that heaven is made with gold and jewels, that it is beautiful, that there will be continuous music, that we will be treated like royalty, that the Church will celebrate victory with magnificent feasts and the sumptuous marriage supper of the Lamb.

But the Holy Spirit goes beyond describing heaven as an improvement of what we enjoy here. We will also have justice and righteousness in heaven. Most of all, there will be joy.

—John Donne: *Sermons*

# FEBRUARY
## *Attentiveness to the Spirit*

FEBRUARY 1

## Spiritual Perception

We do not perceive with logic the basic truths upon which our being rests. We are aware of them mystically. This faculty of spiritual apprehension (so different from what we learn in schools and colleges) must be educated and fed. It needs more careful training than our lower faculties, or it will starve and die even as we gain increased knowledge of other subjects.

The tools for teaching it are reverent thought, meditation, and prayer. These feed the soul.

—John Shairp
*Hindrances to Spiritual Growth*

FEBRUARY 2

## Aware

Even the most primitive person has some idea of God. The purpose of our creation is that we may know the majesty of our Creator. Our business is to know God, and to love him above all else. Awe and reverence are our way of honoring God.

The principle work of our attention is to seek God, to affectionately desire God, and to settle down nowhere else other than in God.

—John Calvin: *Instruction in Faith*

FEBRUARY 3

## *Self-Examination*

My Bible was my guide by day and my pillow by night during my captivity. A comforting Scripture caught my attention. "For a brief moment I abandoned you, but with deep compassion I will bring you back" (Isaiah 54:7). In this way the Lord sustained me.

There were many despondent days. "I cried like a swift or thrush, I moaned like a mourning dove. My eyes grew weak as I looked to the heavens. I am troubled; O Lord, come to my aid!" (Isaiah 38:14). I had time for self-examination. My conscience did not accuse me of anything I ever did toward others. Still, I saw that my walk with God had been careless. I knew I needed God's mercy.

I remembered how we used to gather as a family on Saturday and Sunday nights, often including other kin and neighbors. We would pray and sing, have a good meal, and have a comfortable bed to lie down on. Now I have only a little swill for the body, and like a pig, must lie down on the ground. I was like the prodigal who "longed to fill his stomach with the pods that the pigs were eating, but no one gave him anything" (Luke 15:16). It is impossible to tell you how much sorrow was in my spirit. The Lord knows it. A comforting Scripture would often come into my mind. "For a brief moment I abandoned you, but with deep compassion I will bring you back" (Isaiah 54:7).

—Mary Rowlandson
*Narrative of Captivity and Restoration*

FEBRUARY 4

## Religious Ecstasy

Some who have been subjects of the Spirit of God have been in a kind of ecstasy. Carried away, they enjoy strong imaginations. It is as though they had a heavenly vision and see glorious sights. I am acquainted with such instances. I see no reason to attribute them to the devil. Neither are they the equivalent of prophet's visions or St. Paul's rapture into paradise. The explanation is in human nature.

It is possible to give such moments a wrong interpretation and lay too much weight on them. But yet, I believe that such things are sometimes from the Spirit of God, though the imaginations that attend them are accidental, confused, improper and false.

—Jonathan Edwards
*Marks of a Work of the True Spirit*


FEBRUARY 5

## It Can't be Taught

Clear and trained intellect is one thing; spiritual discernment quite another. They are energies of two different sides of our being. Unless our spiritual nature is alive and active, we work in vain at religious truth merely from the intellectual side. If you are not awake in a deeper region than the intellectual, you will not be a vital theologian or a religious person. Only a devout person can speculate about God because only such a person has the original data.

The soul is larger than the mind.

—John Shairp
*Hindrances to Spiritual Growth*

FEBRUARY 6

## *Discerning our Entitlement*

The people of God have a glorious promise. Why do so many of us live without being sure of this? We are willing to live with uncertainty. Are we awake or asleep? What are we thinking about? Where are our hearts?

If we had a case in court, we would be careful to know whether it will go for or against us. If we were being tried for our lives, we would be very diligent to do everything possible to keep from being condemned. If we were seriously ill, we would ask the doctor, "Will I live or die?" But in the business of our salvation, we are willing to be uncertain.

The reason most people will give for the hope that is in them is, "God is merciful, and Christ died for sinners." Anyone can speak such generalities. Ask them to prove their interest in Christ and the saving mercy of God, and they can tell you nothing. They would shrug as Cain did. "Am I my soul's keeper?"

—Richard Baxter
*The Saint's Everlasting Rest*

FEBRUARY 7

## *Honest Experience*

My sister said, "Look up, children, the Master is coming! Turn me around, and let me die in the arms of Jesus; for I shall soon be with him in glory." We turned her over, as she requested, and waited for her death.

What will infidelity say to this? It surely will not attempt to charge a sincere Christian on her deathbed with hypocrisy. Neither is it fanaticism. These experiences, under certain circumstances, are the natural result of the exercise of Christian faith. The subject is worthy of intensive study. The vast variety of religious experiences of all lively Christians, in every grade of society, in all ages, and in all denominations and sections of the Christian Church, are of too uniform and definite a character to be a result of the wild and fluctuating uncertainties of fanaticism. There is widespread uniformity in the genuine pilgrim's progress of Christian experience, while allowing for great variety of individual features. These are stubborn facts that go beyond reason.

—Zilpha Elaw: *Memoirs*


FEBRUARY 8

## *Marks of the Spirit*

Do not judge the activity of God's Spirit by any effects on our bodies. Tears, trembling, groans, loud outcries, agonies, and failing strength are not indicators. The influence persons are under is not to be evaluated one way or the other by such physical effects. Scripture does not give us any rule for this. We cannot conclude that persons are under the influence of the true Spirit because we see such effects upon their bodies. On the other hand, we have no reason to conclude that the Spirit of God does not influence such outward appearances. We simply cannot tell.

—Jonathan Edwards
*Marks of a Work of the True Spirit*


FEBRUARY 9

## *Psalm 139*

O Lord in me, there is naught
    but to your search revealed lies
        for when I sit
          you notice it
    no less you notice when I rise
the closest closet of my thought
    has open windows to your eyes.

You walk with me, when I walk,
    when to my bed for rest I go
        I find you there
        and everywhere
    not youngest thought in me does grow
No not one word I dare to talk
    But yet unuttered you do know.

> If forth I march, you go before
> If back I turn, you come behind;
> So forth nor back
> your guard I lack
> Always on me your hand I find
> Well I your wisdom may adore
> But never reach with earthly mind.
>
> —Mary Sidney: *The Sidney Psalter*

FEBRUARY 10

## Standing Pat

Any discerning person who completely subscribes to a religious system is often forced to do violence to his own understanding. He loses the benefit of his own discretion and must reconcile his reason to his guide. There are persons of great understanding who are completely subject to the authority of their church. It is amusing to see them sweat while defending some point they don't agree with, but believe they must because the church has said it. Instead of believing the truth as they perceive it, they can only confirm the position of the guide. If any argument against an article of their faith seems unanswerable, they take it for a temptation rather than an illumination. They think the devil is the author of what God's Spirit has helped them to find. The Pharisees felt this way about Jesus.

—Jeremy Taylor: *The Liberty of Prophesying*

FEBRUARY 11

## Hidden

Beneath Christian activity lies a secluded and hidden life. While we ought to be strong and vigorous as we work for the kingdom of God, we have at the same time an unknown and hidden life unrecognized by the world.

We do not display our inner religious experience. The risen Christ revealed himself only to his own. We will share our personal inner life only with those who share our faith. This does not mean we will form separate little groups. In the days of our Lord's resurrection there were various kinds of experiences, but one common inner fellowship connected everyone together. Even those who as yet had experienced nothing were not sent away empty. They were led gently and gradually into the new life.

—Friedrich Schleiermacher: *Selected Sermons*

FEBRUARY 12

## Getting Our Attention

Moses was alone before the burning bush. He had no companion. It is often true that we are never less alone than with God. We may want someone else with us, but happy persons are the ones who can say, "Lord, your company is enough." Moses was startled at the sight, and it completely absorbed his attention. "Though the bush was on fire it did not burn up"

(Exodus 3:2). The phenomenon was intended to startle him. When God intends to speak, he will first gain the attention of the listener. "I will go over and see this strange sight" (Exodus 3:3). It was an uncommon, but glorious sight. I pray God, you and I may see it with faith.

—George Whitefield: *Memoirs*

FEBRUARY 13

## Naturally Spiritual

I do not believe that painful questionings and violent mental convulsions are an ordeal which all thoughtful persons need to experience. Some of the finest spirits, those whose vision is intuitive and penetrating, are the most exempt from anxious soul-searching. Doubts never trouble some at all. They find enough in their faith to feed their spiritual life. They do not need to inquire into the foundations of belief. A power within their hearts inspires them. The heavenly side of all truths is so clear to them that any doubts about the human form of it are either not perceived or ignored. They grow in knowledge by quiet, steady increase of light, without any intervals of darkness and difficulty.

Anyone who can believe without the evidence of sense or labored argument is in the most blessed condition. Their spirits are in such harmony with the truth that the moment they see it, they accept it.

—John Shairp: *Hindrances to Spiritual Growth*

FEBRUARY 14

## Soul Music

The Holy Spirit of God can tune and play our souls like a musical instrument. The result is an increased harmony of divine praise, thanksgiving, and adoration, which arises from a symphony of instruments and voices. To condemn this variety in God's people, or to be upset with those who play a different instrument, is a clear sign that we are spiritually undeveloped.

—William Law: *Mystical Writings*


FEBRUARY 15

## We Never Did it That Way

What the church has been used to is not a rule by which we are to judge. There may be new and extraordinary works of God. In the past, God has worked in unexpected ways. He has made new things happen and performed strange works. God surprises both people and angels. The work of the Spirit was in a manner that was altogether new. We have no reason to think that God will not continue to act this way. We should not limit God where he has not limited himself.

It is not reasonable to determine that a work is not from God's Holy Spirit because of the extraordinary degree of influence on human minds. We naturally are suspicious of things that are unfamiliar. The older we get the more we are suspicious of anything untried and unreported in the past.

—Jonathan Edwards
*Marks of a Work of the Spirit of God*

FEBRUARY 16

## *Christ's Attentive Spirit*

Indications of Christ's divine love are his conversations with God. He delighted in prayer. He would frequently turn aside from the world. With the greatest devotion and pleasure he would spend whole nights in prayer.

He had no sins to confess. He had only a few secular interests to pray for. His whole life was a kind of prayer—a constant communion with God. He kept the fire burning even when there was no sacrifice to offer. The blessed Jesus was never surprised by that dullness, or coolness of spirit, which often makes our devotion weak.

—Henry Scougal
*The Life of God in the Soul of Man*

FEBRUARY 17

## *Remaining Connected*

We are too complex and imperfect to have a totally spiritual religious experience that is out of touch with the world. In all the history of our faith there have been only a few transcendent spirits. They seem to have lived with the angels far above the ordinary world. These exceptional people are not realistic models for most of the rest of us. The important thing is to blend devotion with useful activity among others. This will have a greater effect on the world.

—Hannah More: *Practical Piety*

FEBRUARY 18

## *Revealing Light*

Deal plainly with yourself. Let the eternal light search you and test you. It will deal plainly with you. It will rip you up, lay you open, and reveal everything that is in you. The subtle spiritual activity of your soul's enemy will not remain secret. Come to the light and be searched, judged, and guided.

—Margaret Fell Fox
*Epistle to Convinced Friends, 1653*

FEBRUARY 19

## *Spiritual Deafness*

A bell does not have the ability to hear its own sound. It receives no benefit from its stroke. "If I speak in the tongues of men and of angels, but have not love, I am only a resounding gong or a clanging cymbal" (1 Corinthians 13:1). The preacher who lacks love doesn't understand anything he says. The speaker is not improved. Knowledge needs to be placed in the service

of love. It is far better to be a poor speaker than to speak as an angel while seeking one's own interests.
—Martin Luther: *Sermon on Christian Love*

FEBRUARY 20

## *An Important Question*
"Did you receive the Holy Spirit when you believed?" (Acts 19:2). Do you have the seal of the truth of Christ's doctrine in yourself? Everyone who takes Christianity seriously needs to ask whether or not we have received the Holy Spirit. The Spirit is promised to all believers, but many are deceived. They think they have received the Holy Spirit when they have not. "Each tree is recognized by its own fruit" (Luke 6:44). Do we produce "the fruit of the Spirit"? (Galatians 5:22). Are we led by the Spirit? Do we walk in the Spirit? Are we under the government of the Spirit?
—Matthew Henry
*Commentary on the Whole Bible*

FEBRUARY 21

## *Sacred Navigation*
A ship's captain uses the North Star to plot his course upon the sea. We, who are passengers and strangers in this world, must look to God. If we will do that, no storm will capsize us. We will be guided past dangers and arrive safely at our haven of rest. Jesus said, "I am

the light of the world. Whoever follows me will never walk in darkness, but will have the light of life" (John 8:12).

—John Jewell: *Of the Holy Scriptures*

FEBRUARY 22

## Soul in Residence

Humans are a compound, a mixture of flesh and spirit. The soul, during its residence in the body, acts through the inferior capacity of the flesh. Our Savior Christ took upon himself all of our natural weakness, "yet was without sin" (Hebrews 4:15). He wept and experienced sorrow. He was moved to pity and became angry. These things show that there might be gall in a dove, passion without sin, fire without smoke, and motion without disturbance. It is not the agitation, but the sediment at the bottom, that clouds the water. When it is windy and dusty, the wind does not make, but only raises the dust.

—Robert South: *The Image of God in Man*

FEBRUARY 23

## Church Leadership

"When Jesus landed and saw a large crowd, he had compassion on them, because they were like sheep without a shepherd" (Mark 6:34). If sheep were not inclined to stray, why would they need a shepherd? If little children could guide themselves, why would they need parents? If the vine did not hang down, and lie on the ground, what need would it have of arbors and pruning? If there were no fear for the passage of a ship, why would it need a captain?

The Church is not invulnerable. It makes mistakes. It is not immune to decay from within. The Church needs a Shepherd, a Father, a Vinedresser, and a Captain.

—John Jewell: *Exposition on the Thessalonians*

FEBRUARY 24

## *Duality*

Jesus was truly human. He took our nature. Don't think there could be one Jesus Christ who is God and another Jesus Christ who is human. God allows the heresies that troubled the church in the past to stir up our times also. Jesus was "tempted in every way, just as we are—yet was without sin" (Hebrews 4:15).

We have two eyes, each working independently. But when we look at something, our separate sight is joined together and becomes one. Our sight concentrates on seeing what is before us. In the same way, there are two diverse natures in Jesus Christ.

Is there anything more different than body and soul? The body has properties which are entirely different from those of the soul. If God used such workmanship on us when two different qualities were united, why should we think it strange that God performed a far greater miracle in Jesus Christ?

—John Calvin: *The Mystery of Godliness*

FEBRUARY 25

## *The Beginning*

Many make the mistake of plunging into a religious life without starting at the right place. We need to begin with a necessary basic conviction. Start with the understanding that our nature is alienated from God. It is not a matter of having a little blemish. We are fallen creatures. We not only need to be improved, we need a complete change of heart.

—Hannah More: *Practical Piety*

FEBRUARY 26

## *Love*

Love is our greatest asset. Love is the only thing we can really call our own. Other things can be taken away from us by force, but nothing is strong enough to destroy our love. By giving our love, we give everything. It is not possible to refuse to yield ourselves to the object of our love. By giving our love we give ourselves. Love is the worthiest present we can offer God.

—Henry Scougal
*The Life of God in the Soul of Man*

FEBRUARY 27

## *The Purpose*

There is a reason for spiritual gifts. "To each one the manifestation of the Spirit is given for the common good" (1 Corinthians 12:7). They are not distributed for the honor and advantage of those who have them. They are for the benefit of the church. They are to help spread and advance the gospel. God provides us with the ability to do something for others. These gifts are to be used for the glory of God.

—Matthew Henry
*Commentary on the Whole Bible*


FEBRUARY 28

## *Repentance*

Repentance is not the paying of a penalty imposed by a judge. Repentance is facing the truth about yourself. When Christ tells us to "repent," he is not speaking of a feigned repentance sometimes prescribed by the church that gives you a license to sin. Jesus means we are to go into ourselves, investigating the reasons for our behavior. When we do this honestly, we are awakened to a new life. Those who responded to this awakening received the sacrament of baptism. They gave public testimony that they were going to begin a life quite unlike the one they had lived previously.

—Ulrich Zwingli: *On True and False Religion*

FEBRUARY 29

## *Ordinary Members*

The Church is very much like the burning bush Moses saw. Why wasn't it a tall cedar or some other large, glorious tree? Why did God choose a bush, a little bush of briars and thorns?

The Church generally consists of poor, ordinary, disgraceful people. It may be glorious at its center, but it is not very attractive outwardly. When the Church prospered under Constantine, it was hugged to death. The great poet Milton noted that when the emperor gave ministers rich vestments, high honors, great livings, and golden pulpits, the Church actually deteriorated. Favoritism poisoned the Church.

God's people are like a little bramble bush. Jesus Christ does this with the intention of confounding the world.

—George Whitefield: *Memoirs*

## MARCH
# *With God in Difficult Times*

MARCH 1

## Rough Road Ahead

Be willing to travel any road God commands. Some will be easy and others difficult, seemingly against our own best interests. The way to heaven ascends. We must agree to travel uphill. It will be hard and tiresome. It will contradict every natural predisposition we have. We won't want to do it.

Follow Christ on the path he traveled. This is the way to heaven. "If any want to be my followers, let them deny themselves and take up their cross and follow me" (Matthew 16:24 NRSV). Follow Christ in meekness and lowliness of heart, obedience and love. Be diligent to do good, and patient under afflictions.

—Jonathan Edwards: *Works*


MARCH 2

## Taken Captive

About sunrise on February 10, 1675, many Indians fell upon Lancaster. "Come and see the works of the LORD, the desolations he has brought on the earth" (Psalm 46:8). It is a solemn sight to see so many Christians lying in their blood, some here, and some there, like a flock of sheep torn by wolves. Yet the Lord preserved a few of us from death. They captured twenty-four of us and took us away.

The next day was Sunday. I remembered how careless I had been of God's holy time. I had thrown

Sundays away. Yet the Lord had mercy on me and kept me going. If he wounded me with one hand, he healed me with the other.

—Mary Rowlandson
*Narrative of Captivity and Restoration*

MARCH 3

## God Will Help

Clouds return after rain. Life is marked with good times and bad. Cloudy days attend the most prosperous periods of life. It is always darkest just before daybreak. Our trouble usually becomes God's opportunity.

When Moses stood before the burning bush [Exodus 3:2-3] his people were slaves. They had been slaves in Egypt for many long years. It seemed that God had forgotten them. When the time God had determined came, he delivered his people from bondage. God defeated all opposition.

—George Whitefield: *Memoirs*

MARCH 4

## Hurts that Help

Afflictions test us. Gold is not worse when it is tried by fire, or wheat for being winnowed. Adversity is God's fan and his sieve. It tests our mettle.

Some use religion for their own advantage. They are like a fisherman who uses nets only to catch fish.

They use the net of religion only to catch preferment. Difficulties will reveal who they are. Hypocrites do not sail in a storm. Winter does not exhaust true grace. A precious faith is like the star that shines brightest in the darkest night.

Difficult times purge us. No one is so good that they do not need purification. The brightest day has its clouds. The purest gold contains dross. The most refined soul still has some dregs of corruption. The saints lose nothing in the furnace other than the dross they can spare. Plowing cultivates the soil. We refer to a "harrowing event." Harrowing the earth breaks up hard clods and prepares it for bearing fruit.

—Thomas Watson: *The Art of Divine Contentment*

MARCH 5

## *Fatherly Advice*

A good and loving father will give his son sound advice before sending him on a risky trip. He will instruct him in ways to avoid peril. Watch out for this! Be careful of that! Bad things have happened along your route. Be careful.

If a father is that concerned about worldly dangers, why not point out spiritual hazards? He should tell his child to watch out for the snares that wait in life, and to be strong in the faith, seeking God's help through life's difficulties.

—John Jewell: *Exposition on the Thessalonians*

MARCH 6

## Resisting Evil

As bullets are always a danger to soldiers, so are we always within the reach of temptation. We serve God when we avoid forbidden behavior, as well as when we do what is right. It is a better service to God to resist a temptation to evil than to offer many formal prayers.

Would you serve God? Then watch carefully for temptation. God is present. God is the overseer of all your behavior and private thoughts.

—William Penn: *Some Fruits of Solitude*


MARCH 7

## Others Have Been Here

"As an example of patience in the face of suffering, take the prophets who spoke in the name of the Lord" (James 5:10). The prophets, on whom God put the greatest honor and favor, were the most afflicted. The best have had the hardest time in this world. Notice that those who are the greatest examples of suffering are also the best examples of patience. "We consider blessed those who have persevered. You have heard of Job's perseverance and have seen what the Lord finally brought about. The Lord is full of compassion and mercy" (James 5:11). The best way to bear afflictions is to look to the end of them. Let us serve our God, and endure our trials, as those who believe the end will crown everything.

—Matthew Henry: *Commentary on the Whole Bible*

MARCH 8

## Psalm 71

On you my trust is grounded.
Lord let me never be
>   With shame confounded
>   But set me free
And in your justice rescue me
Your gracious care to my way bend
>   And me defend.

Be you my rock and my tower
My ever safe resort
>   Whose saving power
>   Has not been short
To work my safety, for my fort
On you alone is built; in you
>   My strongholds be.

Mary Sidney: *The Sidney Psalter*

MARCH 9

## Letter from Prison

The Lord be with you. My hope is in the mercy of Jesus Christ, that he will grant me his spirit and help me cling to the truth. Pray to the Lord for me. "The spirit is willing, but the body is weak" (Matthew 26:41).

It was a joy to take the hand of Seignior John, who did not hesitate to offer it to a condemned heretic, in chains. Paletz visited me in prison and told me that I was the most dangerous heretic since Wycliffe. He said my sermons had infected everyone who has listened to me. I told him he was cruel. I was going to be burned at the stake in the morning. A verse of Scripture remains in my mind. "Do not put your trust in princes" (Psalm 146:3).

—John Huss: *Letter to Friends*

MARCH 10

## *Death*

Though death is a dark passage, it leads to immortality. Faith illumines the darkness, giving evidence of things not seen. The knowledge that the grave is not the end is a source of comfort. We live as soon as we die. Death is no more than a turning from time to eternity. Death is a part of life. We cannot love to live if we cannot bear to die.

—William Penn: *Some Fruits of Solitude*

MARCH 11

## *The Greatest Affliction of All*

I was now left alone in the world, with two infant children. I had no other dependence than the promise: "A father to the fatherless, a defender of widows, is God in his holy dwelling" (Psalm 68:5). God gave me friends who generously comforted me. I can say with the psalmist: "I was young and now I am old, yet I have never seen the righteous forsaken or their children begging bread" (Psalm 37:25). I have been fed by his bounty, clothed by his mercy, comforted and healed when sick, succored when tempted, and everywhere upheld by his hand.

—Jarena Lee: *Life and Religious Experience*

MARCH 12

## Ending Winter

The best way to have peace and security is to have a good spiritual life. Countries far to the north are cold and icy because they are a greater distance from the sun. We can shiver because we are too far from heaven.

Sunshine in spring awakens the earth. Grass becomes green, buds on tree limbs open, dormant plants come to life, and birds begin to sing. Nature wears a smile. If we lived close to God, keeping our thoughts on heavenly things, a spring of joy would rise within us. We would forget the sorrows of winter. We would wake up and sing praises to God.

—Richard Baxter: *The Saints' Everlasting Rest*

MARCH 13

## A Severe Mercy

I had been under this dark cloud for more than three weeks. It felt more like three months. Now it was gone. Heaven again opened to my eyes and ears because at last I discerned the path of obedience. I listened to God's counsel: "This is the way; walk in it" (Isaiah 30:21). The chastisement of God is often more profitable than his indulgence would be. His correction is kindness, and his severity mercy.

—Zilpha Elaw: *Memoirs*

MARCH 14

## *A Prayer for Difficult Times*

Thank you, God, for my trouble. Thank you for putting me into these afflictions one after another. I thought I could have a little rest, but trouble came to me from the very place I would have expected to receive comfort. "I do believe; help me overcome my unbelief!" (Mark 9:24). I will go on praising you, my God, to all eternity. You will transform this unpleasantness into something beautiful.

—George Whitefield: *Memoirs*

MARCH 15

## *Off the Beaten Path*

Long journeys are fatiguing. This is particularly true when the trail goes through a wilderness. Anyone traveling in rough country expects to suffer hardships and weariness. This is the way it is on the way of holiness. We will need to surmount difficulties and obstacles that are in the way. The land we have to travel through is a wilderness. There are many mountains, rocks, and rough places that we must go over. It is necessary that we expend our strength.

Start the trip early. As soon as you become capable of doing something for yourself, let this be your first concern. Set your course for *this* journey. Let it be the work of every day. Keep your destination in mind. Head in that direction as long as you live.

—Jonathan Edwards: *Works*

MARCH 16

## Christ's Difficult Time

Christ's sufferings glorify him. His native luster shines brightly in his last difficult hour on earth. He knows about the cross, the scourge, the nails, and the spear. But his soul was not overcome. Distress brings nobility to every great character. Distress glorifies the Son of God. By his example, he teaches all of us how to suffer and die.

Everything he said during this time was magnanimous. Herod's court, Pilate's judgment hall, and Calvary were like theaters where he could display all the virtues of a constant and patient mind. To the last moment of his life we see a gentle and benevolent spirit. No upbraiding, no complaining escaped his lips during his cruel death. With all the dignity of a sovereign he conferred pardon on a fellow sufferer. With greatness beyond example, he spent his last moments in apologies and prayers for those who were shedding his blood.

—Hugh Blair<br>*The Hour and the Event of all Time*

MARCH 17

## Inscription of Love

"Trials must and will befall;
  But with humble faith to see,
 Love inscribed upon them all,
  This is happiness to me."

The smiles of Jesus sweetened my bitter cup. I was able to work easily because my heavenly Father took the heaviest end of the cross and bore it with me.

—Zilpha Elaw: *Memoirs*

MARCH 18

## Trouble

"Our light and momentary troubles are achieving for us an eternal glory that far outweighs them all" (2 Corinthians 4:17). Anything that works for my glory in heaven works for my good. Scripture does not tell us that our honor and riches work for us a weight of glory. The heavier the trouble, the greater the glory. Our troubles do not *earn* us any glory. Instead of being the cause of glory, they are the way to glory. It was the same way with Christ. "It was fitting that God . . . in bringing many children to glory, should make the author of their salvation perfect through sufferings" (Hebrews 2:10).

—Thomas Watson
*The Art of Divine Contentment*

MARCH 19

# High Hopes

Human life is ordinarily little else than a collection of disappointments. Things rarely turn out the way we hope. We often fail. We work at jobs we did not intend to do. Even the place we live is often different from the place we imagined. Still more different is the success that follows our efforts.

We all intend to be rich and honorable, to enjoy ease and to pursue pleasure. The smallest minority of us accomplish these things. Most of us are competent, but few are rich. Many of us have reputable character, but honor comes to only a limited number. Most of us stop at a moderate level. Human efforts appear to have their boundary established in the determination of God. "I know, O Lord, that the way of human beings is not in their control, that mortals as they walk cannot direct their steps" (Jeremiah 10:23 NRSV).

—Timothy Dwight: *The Sovereignty of God*

MARCH 20

## *Share Christ's Burden*

Many complain against God for a lack of support. They think it is odd that God allows his children to be stepped on by the ungodly. It would be enough to answer that God is in charge and knows best. But when we can discover Jesus Christ in the pattern of events that trouble us, then we may consider it an honor to share his burden. "Greatly rejoice, though now for a little while you may have to suffer grief in all kinds of trials. These have come so that your faith—of greater worth than gold, which perishes even though refined by fire—may be proved genuine and may result in praise, glory and honor" (1 Peter 1:6f).

—John Calvin: *Enduring Persecution for Christ*


MARCH 21

## *Trusting Honors God*

"Love is patient . . . always trusts, always hopes, always perseveres" (1 Corinthians 13:4, 7). It is clear that fuming and anger have no part of love. When we are sick or having a time of adversity, our duty is to be patient and to suffer willingly. Call upon Christ for help and comfort. Without him we will not be able to persevere. God has promised to help. The greatest way we can dishonor God is by not believing or trusting him. Be patient, trusting, and believe that God will deliver us when it seems good to him. God knows the time better than we do.

—Hugh Latimer: *On Christian Love*

MARCH 22

## Misery and Mercy

No matter how many miseries you have, the Lord has many mercies for you. God deals with us as a father deals with a son who has been sent on a business trip. The weather turns foul. A dangerous storm arises. The father pities the great difficulties his son is facing. He is eager to see him return home. He makes great preparations to welcome and entertain him. His one thought is to do something good for his child.

It is the same way with God. We need to find our way through many troubles and griefs. Don't be discouraged. The more misery, the greater God's mercy. He is watching over you.

—Thomas Hooker: *The Activity of Faith*

MARCH 23

## Above the Fray

Offer yourself completely to God. Let your love derive from his love. Let your soul rest and delight in being melted into God. Let such an experience reassure you. Then you will not feel any real difference between honor and shame, joy and sorrow. You will welcome whatever you know that has to do with the honor of your Lord. It will not matter if it is difficult or unpleasant for you. You will embrace it. You will desire it. When you have done all that is possible for you to do, you will think you have done nothing. You will be sorry you have served your Lord so imperfectly.

—Robert Leighton
*Rules and Instructions for a Holy Life*

MARCH 24

## Christ's Agony

Jesus endured the sharpest of all afflictions and extreme misery. He never uttered a negative thought or complaint. He felt it all. He had as quick a sense of pain as anyone else. He understood the depth of his spiritual suffering. "And being in anguish, he prayed more earnestly, and his sweat was like drops of blood falling to the ground" (Luke 22:44). Still, he willingly accepted it.

"Now is my heart troubled, and what shall I say? 'Father, save me from this hour'? No, it was for this very reason I came to this hour. Father, glorify your name!" (John 12:27-28). We see the inconceivable weight and pressure he was to bear. He could not think of it without terror. But considering the glory of God he was not only willing to suffer it, he desired to suffer.

—Henry Scougal
*The Life of God in the Soul of Man*

MARCH 25

## *Prayer in Time of Trouble*

My Lady's footman, Thomas Petty, brought me letters from Westmoreland. They informed me how gravely ill my dear mother was. She was not able to write to me herself. Those who were attending her did not expect her to recover. At night I went out and prayed to God, my only helper, asking that she might not die.

The next day Richard Jones came from London and brought a letter that stated unless I surrendered my family property, conducting the business as my husband desired, I would be in great difficulty.

After dinner Mr. Oberton and I had a long conversation. He told me how much others condemned me. Most people could not understand my reluctance to part with my estates. I kneeled in prayer and asked God to send a good end to this troublesome business. I completely trusted God. He has always helped me.

—Anne Clifford: *Diary*


MARCH 26

## *No Immunity*

Faith is more precious than gold. Gold is tried by fire. We may suffer for our Lord. Let there be no complaint if that is our assignment. Christ suffered for us. We can follow in his footsteps. Jesus said, "Blessed are you when people insult you, persecute you and falsely say all kinds of evil against you because of me. Rejoice and be glad, because great is your reward in heaven, for in the same way they persecuted the prophets who were before you" (Matthew 5:11-12).

If Christ suffered, why should we expect to be spared? Be confident that your heavenly Father wishes good for you. Cast all your care upon God. He will give you what is best.

—Nicholas Ridley: *Farewell*

MARCH 27

## *Effective Teachers*

Trouble and affliction are the best teachers. How can we experience God's goodness if nothing ever threatens us? It is when we are in great danger that God can help. If our health is perfect we do not seek a doctor.

This is why God sometimes teaches severe lessons to those he loves most dearly. Troubles and risks are effective schoolmasters. An ancient Greek proverb contends that wisdom can be struck into a student. We are never more holy than when we bear a dreadful cross.

—John Fox
*Christ Jesus Triumphant*

MARCH 28

## *Pride*

Whoever has a high regard for personal merits usually has a low regard for his circumstances. A proud person is a discontented person.

If you think you are better than other people, you will find fault with the wisdom of God. You will think you should be above others. The creature dares to criticize its Creator. "Shall what is formed say to him who formed it, 'Why did you make me like this?' Does not the potter have the right to make out of the same lump of clay some pottery for noble purposes and some for common use?" (Romans 9:20-21).

Discontent is nothing other than the boiling over of pride.

—Thomas Watson: *The Art of Divine Contentment*


MARCH 29

## *One of Us*

The apostle says that Jesus "had to become like his brothers and sisters in every respect, so that he might be a merciful and faithful high priest in the service of God, to make a sacrifice of atonement for the sins of the people. Because he himself was tested by what he suffered, he is able to help those who are being tested" (Hebrews 2:17-18 NRSV). If we are not acquainted with adversity, we do not have compassion for others. If we are living in luxury, we have little understanding of poverty.

Our Lord Jesus Christ participated in human life. He experienced all our miseries. When we come to him, he is ready to help, because he knows what our afflictions are actually like. He asks God to have pity on us.

—John Calvin: *The Only Mediator*

MARCH 30

## *A Great Voyage*

Life has been compared with an ocean, and our progress though it a voyage. The ocean is tempestuous and billowy. The sky over it is stormy. There are shoals and reefs beneath the surface. The trip is adventurous and full of uncertainty. It has always been this way. The present, and that part of the past you know by experience, confirms it.

—Timothy Dwight: *The Sovereignty of God*

MARCH 31

## *Proper Prayer*

There will be many occasions for spontaneous prayer every day. Something will be out of control in your life. You will learn of difficulties some other person is facing. If you are experiencing healthy and prosperous times, you can offer a prayer of thanksgiving and sing God's praise.

Never attempt to confine God to your personal circumstances. Don't limit his action to a particular span of time. God will act when, where, and how he will. These are not for us to dictate. Instead of imposing conditions on the manner in which God may answer your prayer, leave it to his good judgment.

Before you ask for anything specific, honestly pray that God's "will be done" (Matthew 6:10). Place what you desire beneath what God desires. Let that action curb your desires.

—John Calvin: *Of Prayer*

≈§ APRIL
*Mystery of God*

APRIL 1
## Beyond Words

The majesty of God goes beyond the capacity of human understanding. We cannot fully comprehend God. Our task is to adore rather than to investigate.

Since the splendor of God is overwhelming, we will do better to look for God in his works. "For since the creation of the world God's invisible qualities—his eternal power and divine nature—have been clearly seen, being understood from what has been made, so that men are without excuse" (Romans 1:20). This does not keep our intellect up in the air through frivolous and vain speculations.

Faith and reverence will nourish our spiritual life.

—John Calvin: *Instruction in Faith*

APRIL 2
## God Is

It is impossible to take God anyplace he is not already present. "The kingdom of God is within you" (Luke 17:21). It does not come to someone who looks for it outside himself. The person who really seeks God already has God. Without God we can neither seek nor find God.

—Hans Denck: *Writings*

APRIL 3

## Awed by God

Lord, you have promised your love. Why do I doubt it? You created me; I am your creature. You are my master; I am your servant. You are my Father; I am your child. "I will be a Father to you, and you will be my sons and daughters, says the Lord Almighty" (2 Corinthians 6:19). If this were not enough, God is also my husband. Even more, I am a member of his body, the church.

These thoughts stagger me. God has done so much for me and I have returned so little. I take comfort in the fact that when I arrive in heaven, I will understand all of this perfectly. Then I will be able to praise God properly.

—Anne Bradstreet: *Works of Anne Bradstreet*

APRIL 4

## God's Place

The world represents a rare and sumptuous palace. We are God's family living in it. God is the Lord and master of it all.

What a luxurious place this! Many glorious luminaries adorn the heavens. The earth has its groves, plains, valleys, hills, fountains, ponds, lakes, and rivers. It produces a variety of fruits and creatures for food, pleasure, and profit. How noble a house God keeps! There is such abundance and variety on his excellent table. There is an impressive orderliness of the seasons and the suitableness of every time and thing.

We are careless servants. We do not take care of God's bounty. He has patience with us and forgives us. He has not yet broken the house and sent us out to take care of ourselves.

But though God has stocked this world with an abundance of good things for our life and comfort, they remain imperfect goods. They merely point to God who is the only perfect good. Sadly, we cannot see God because of all these material things. We need to look for God in them.

—William Penn: *Some Fruits of Solitude*

APRIL 5

## Greater than We Think

Thought falls short of the highest truth when law controls it. We hesitate to go up beyond natural and moral law to God. Some think that when science has ascended to the most general ideas, knowledge has reached its limit. Beyond this point all is mere conjecture.

I will not reply to this with the old question about a law and a lawgiver. This may seem like a play on words. The thing to remember is that the perception of ordered phenomena is not necessary. It is an artificial and arbitrarily imposed limitation. Natural thought rebels against it.

Any reflective mind that is not dominated by a system of thought cannot notice the orderliness of it all without asking the origin of that order. What is the arranging power? How did it come to exist?
 —John Shairp: *Hindrances to Spiritual Growth*

APRIL 6
## Results of Love of God
When you love God, you will make every effort to serve and please him. Love is eager to perform good works. Love is alert, energetic and attentive. Faith in God will give you confidence. Hope in God will energize you. Reverence for God will awaken you to new possibilities. Enthusiasm for spiritual things will ignite a fire in you.
 —Richard Baxter: *The Saints' Everlasting Rest*

APRIL 7
## Mystery of the Trinity
Many parts of Scripture are easy to understand, but some parts are truly mysterious. Such passages surpass the utmost limits of human comprehension. While remaining mysteries, they are not absurdities.

One verse clearly represents God as existing in a strange manner. "There are three that bear record in heaven, the Father, the Word, and the Holy Ghost: and these three are one" (1 John 5:7 KJV). This leads us to think of God, the first and Supreme Being, as existing in three distinct persons. I use this word because it is the best our language offers. There is no word in *any* language which can convey a precise idea of this incomprehensible distinction in the divine nature. There is nothing else like it.

Here lies the mystery of the Trinity. Since we can't comprehend it, any attempt to explain it with borrowed comparisons is absurd. Our illustrations obscure rather than elucidate. There is nothing that bears the least resemblance of three persons in one God. "Can you fathom the mysteries of God?" (Job 11:7). All who believe in God must believe mysteries.

—Nathanael Emmons: *Sermons*

APRIL 8

# Distorted Good

Everything about God is good. God is infinitely perfect. There is no way there could be any evil defect in God.

These good qualities can be distorted in imperfect creatures. The creature is limited. The creature can make a mess of things. Strength in the divine nature is the strength of love, and it can never be anything else as long as it is in God. But we can separate this strength from love. Then it becomes evil and we do mischief with it. Good things can be used in an evil way. The only explanation for the existence of evil is that we have become separated from God.

Don't blame God for evil. It would make more sense to blame the sun for darkness.
—William Law: *Mystical Writings*

APRIL 9

## *The Enjoyment of God*

God is our highest good. Enjoyment of God is the only happiness that will satisfy our souls. To fully enjoy God is infinitely better than the most pleasant accommodations here. Fathers and mothers, husbands, wives or children, or the company of earthly friends are but shadows. The enjoyment of God is the substance.

The others are but scattered beams. God is the sun.
The others are but streams. God is the fountain.
The others are but drops. God is the ocean.

Therefore it is beneficial to spend this life only as a journey toward God. Everything else is subordinate to God. Why should we work for, or set our hearts on any other thing than our true happiness?
—Jonathan Edwards: *Works*

APRIL 10

## *Preparation*

God prepared the world, through a long course of ages, for a revolution. The Jewish nation's assignment was to usher it in. One corner of the world preserved

the knowledge of God. In due time that light would spread over the earth. Successive revelations gradually enlarged religious views beyond the narrow boundaries of Judea, to a more extensive kingdom of God. People looked ahead expectantly to this great event. God descended on the flaming mountain. God spoke by the prophet's voice. God scattered his chosen people into captivity and then reassembled them in their own land. God was carrying out a progressive plan which culminated in the death of Christ.
—Hugh Blair: *The Hour and the Event of all Time*


APRIL 11

## Serious About God

Why do you trifle with God? God is eager to hear our prayers and quite willing to give us mercy. God is intimately involved with us. He notices every sigh. When you are in some difficulty you are eager for God's attention. Can you expect real mercies when you ordinarily neglect the Giver of mercies?
—Richard Baxter: *The Saints' Everlasting Rest*


APRIL 12

## Let God Take Control

You cannot direct your own course through the world. Your best plans will often fail. Your expectations will be disappointed. Your fondest dreams will evaporate.

God can direct you. God actually will control all your concerns if you commit yourself to his care. God will direct you kindly and safely. Why do you hesitate to yield yourself and your interests to the guidance of your Maker?

—Timothy Dwight: *The Sovereignty of God*

APRIL 13
## *The Source*
All streams of good have God as their source. God is the sun from which light beams of blessedness flow. Any worthwhile activity results from having God at the center. The rivers and rays of human behavior return to their source in God.

—Hannah More: *Practical Piety*

APRIL 14
## *God in Human Terms*
The Scriptures frequently speak of God as angry because of our sins. There are many descriptions of heated disturbance of God's affection. We are sure these things have no place in God. We need to interpret such passages as human forms of speech. They are an attempt to convey an idea of God's response to our behavior in terms we can easily understand.

We are not to think such expressions signify nothing, that they have no meaning. They simply do not express the same thing we describe in ourselves with these terms. In the divine nature disorder and imperfection do not mar heavenly serenity.

—John Howe
*The Redeemer's Tears Over Lost Souls*

APRIL 15

## *God Returns Love*

God always returns love to a soul that is completely devoted to him and is eager to serve and please him. God cannot scorn his own image or the heart in which it is engraved. Love is the only tribute we can give to God. Love is the sacrifice God will not despise.
—Henry Scougal: *The Life of God in the Soul of Man*

APRIL 16

## *God is Good*

God does not want to harm any creature. There is not, and never has been, a spark of wrath in the holy God. If the wrath of God was ever anywhere, it must be everywhere. If it burned once, it must burn eternally. God cannot be increased or decreased. It would make as much sense to say that God created the universe out of wrath as to say that God ever wrathfully punished any part of it.

God is the unlimited abyss of all that is good. The goodness of God, and a desire to communicate that goodness, inspired creation. God is a constantly overflowing fountain of good. He is love. He gives nothing but the gifts of love.

—William Law: *Mystical Writings*


APRIL 17

## Love and Light

God is love. God's love is infinite and his blessedness is without boundary. If the little love in a good person, offset by sin, sometimes brings unutterable joy, how blessed God must be. The revolt of angels and the misery of human sin do not, for a moment, interrupt the blessedness of God. The events in our world do not surprise God.

Surrounded by unnumbered millions, created by his hand and upheld by his power, God shines forth. What an object of joyful contemplation is the blessedness of God! His boundless capacity is full. It is eternal. The happiness of the created universe is but a drop—a drop that is beyond the reach of trouble. When we look around here below, what we see troubles us. The world can be a wretched place filled with much grief and pain. When we turn our gaze from this scene of darkness and misery, and behold God high above it all, dwelling in light inaccessible and full of glory, the earthly scene brightens. A few rebels who refuse to love and participate in his kindness are groping in darkness on God's footstool, but "God is light; in him there is no darkness at all" (1 John 1:5).

—Lyman Beecher: *Sermons*

APRIL 18

# *Unknowable*

Because our knowledge arrives through the senses, all we know is the surface of things. We perceive color, odor, taste, and other such things. What we know, therefore, is not the actual substance, but its attendant attributes. Reason has little light if it is separated from the body. God has joined soul and body together and it is through the senses that knowledge becomes definite and complete.

The soul's knowledge, however, will not be complete as long as it lives in this mortal body. It will not distinguish the fundamental distinctions and causes of the greater reality. It learns of the inner qualities only through their external qualities. We know God imperfectly. It is not surprising that there is much in God that is a mystery to us. There are many truths of faith that we are not able to prove because there is so much we do not know.

—Girolamo Savonarola: *The Ascension of Christ*

APRIL 19

## The Fullness of God

Infinite and eternal Majesty, author and fountain of existence and blessedness, how little we know of you. We talk of religion and make a pretense at it, but most of us do not know how to serve and please you. We easily mistake the affections of our nature, and issues of self-love, for those divine graces that make us acceptable in your sight.

I am grieved that I have wandered so long, and have been content with vain shadows and false images of piety and religion. I acknowledge and adore your goodness. You have opened my eyes a little and let me see what I should seek. I am pleased to consider the wonderful capacity for improvement you put in my nature. Your light is in me and attracts me closer to you.

—Henry Scougal
*The Life of God in the Soul of Man*


APRIL 20

## Praising God

God does not need our service. God lacks nothing and can do without us. God's divinity is independent of our existence. God created us and all other creatures in order to demonstrate his goodness. Whatever exists is able to sing God's praise.

When we serve others, we serve God. When such service is rendered, God is praised. Each creature has special gifts to be used for the common good.
—Martin Bucer: *Instruction in Christian Love*

APRIL 21
## *God Rules*
God is able to do anything. With a word, he accomplishes what he wants. He said, "'Let there be light,' and there was light" (Genesis 1:3). God can give me peace with a glance. When a storm of thoughts swirl in my head, God can command my soul to be still. All tempests obey him.

The world can frown all it wants as long as God smiles. When God works with me, no problem will ever frighten me.
—Elizabeth Singer Rowe
*Devout Exercises of the Heart*

APRIL 22
## *False Gods*
We can be so attached to something that we turn it into an idol. You may be reluctant to admit it, but you are worshiping a false god. Putting your confidence in anything other than God is idolatry. Wishing you were rich, or wanting the support of a certain person, and thinking that such things will bring you happiness and

security, is having a false god. Our confidence is to be in God alone.

It is even possible to turn the true and living God into an idol. When we attempt to imagine the form and shape of God, we have missed God. Be careful not to create an idol in your heart.

—Thomas Cranmer: *Catechismus*

APRIL 23

## Getting Ready

We should examine and cleanse ourselves before we receive the supper of our Lord Jesus Christ. Then we may be more and more confirmed in his grace, become a part of his body, and be truly made one with him. Understand that he is our life. We live in him and he lives in us. We are God's children.

Earnestly call upon God. Trust in his goodness. Listen to his Word. God would be pleased to show his grace not only to one city or a little handful of people, but also to reign over all the world, that everyone may serve and worship him "in spirit and in truth" (John 4:24).

—John Calvin: *Behavior in the Church*

APRIL 24

## God Forgives

There is no sin too great to be forgiven. Consider your life. Is there any ugliness in you? What will you do?

Ask God to forgive you. He will certainly hear your prayer. Your sins will be forgiven. God will keep his promise. He sent his only Son into the world to save sinners like you. Think of the great love of God the Father. Make improvements in your life. Avoid temptation. If you will do this, no sin in the book will be able to harm or condemn you. God's mercy is greater than the world's sins.

—Hugh Latimer: *Fruitful Sermons*

APRIL 25

## *God in Christ*

All of God's works are unsearchable and beyond human language. The only way we can comprehend God is through faith in Jesus Christ. God came to us in the simplest way. He became one of us, subject to human weakness and death.

—Martin Luther: *Table Talk*

APRIL 26

## *The Greatest Pleasure*

It is an infinite pleasure to be lost in God, to be engulfed in the overwhelming sense of God's goodness. The greatest happiness comes when we can offer ourselves as "living sacrifices" (Romans 12:1), ascending to him in flames of love. There will be no solid joy in a soul until, weary of itself, it abandons itself to the author of its being. Substantial pleasure comes when the soul feels itself becoming a hallowed and devoted thing. Then the soul understands it is sacred, and it will be able to say with feeling and sincerity, "This is my lover, this [is] my friend" (Song of Songs 5:16).

—Henry Scougal
*The Life of God in the Soul of Man*

APRIL 27

## Sin

It is better that God allowed sin rather than prevented it. If God had not permitted us to sin, we would not be free. God would be controlling us against our wills. God can deal with sin, however great it may be. God can, will, and already has overcome it. He has dealt with human sin in a manner that does not harm any of his creatures.

—Hans Denck: *Whether God is the Cause of Evil*

APRIL 28

## Where to Find God

Plato said that God is nothing and yet everything. We are not able to comprehend God. God is invisible to us. Anything we understand and see is not God. God may be seen in his Word and works. If we look for God elsewhere we will take hold of the devil. Let's not flutter too high, but remain by the manger and the swaddling clothes of Christ, "For in Christ all the fullness of the Deity lives in bodily form" (Colossians 2:9). In him we will certainly find God, without seeing, hearing, or feeling.

—Martin Luther: *Table Talk*

APRIL 29

## Search the Scripture

I was greatly troubled while being held captive. Death was as appealing as life. As soon as I could, I read my Bible and came upon a quieting Scripture. "Be still, and know that I am God" (Psalm 46:10). I realized I was facing some difficult times. I sat down in despair, but I was so hungry I could not remain seated. Walking among the trees I found six acorns and two chestnuts which helped a little.

As night approached, I asked them if I could go out alone to gather some sticks to keep me warm. I used this time to pour out my heart unto the LORD. I took my Bible, but could find nothing helpful in it. Sometimes God dries up the streams of comfort. I can report that in all of my sorrow and affliction God did not depart from me. I did not blame God for my trouble. I deserved worse.

Near the end of this sad time I was turning the pages of the Bible and the Lord showed me some passages that helped a little. "'My thoughts are not your thoughts, neither are your ways my ways,' declares the LORD" (Isaiah 55:8). "Commit your way to the LORD; trust in him and he will do this" (Psalm 37:5).

—Mary Rowlandson
*Narrative of Captivity and Restoration*

APRIL 30

## Solid Evidence

We may tire ourselves in a labyrinth of search and talk of God. But if we would really know God, it must be from the impressions we receive of him. The softer our hearts, the deeper and livelier these impressions can be made upon us.

If God has made us aware of his justice by his reproof, of his patience by his forbearance, of his mercy by his forgiveness, of his holiness by touching us with his Spirit, we have a substantial knowledge of God. This is experience rather than speculation. This is enjoyment instead of a report. In short, this is undeniable evidence, with the realities of religion, and will stand all wind and weather.

As our faith, so our devotion should be lively. Cold meat won't serve well at these meals. A coal from God's altar must kindle our fire.

—William Penn: *Some Fruits of Solitude*

# MAY
## Christian Relationships

MAY 1

## A Part of the Whole

Love for others comes before we can pray correctly. God does not want us to be totally independent. We are to be at peace and in harmony with the larger community. Even though we may be alone and pray to God in secret, we must be a part of other faithful believers. Jesus teaches us to pray, "Our Father" (Matthew 6:9). The word *our* binds us together. In this Christian fellowship there is essentially one voice, one heart, one spirit.

Therefore, let all controversy be set aside. Our Lord Jesus Christ says, "If you are offering your gift at the altar and there remember that your brother has something against you, leave your gift there in front of the altar. First go and be reconciled to your brother; then come and offer your gift" (Matthew 5:23–24). Do you seek God's mercy? Be merciful. If we are members of Jesus Christ, his spirit of peace and unity will govern us. Live in friendship and love if you desire to be welcomed when you approach God.

—John Calvin: *The Privilege of Prayer*

MAY 2

## Helping Others

Christian love produces a sincere love and affection for others. "Truly I tell you, just as you did it to one of the least of these who are members of my family, you did it to me" (Matthew 25:40 NRSV). This comment deeply impresses us. We look for opportunities to express our gratitude to Christ by helping others.

Loving fellow Christians is easy enough. We enjoy being together and sharing similar ideas and purposes. While it is difficult to take pleasure in secular society, we can still sincerely want to help those who are not Christian. Perhaps our behavior will communicate our love for Jesus. Others may be attracted to Christ. Consequently, we will not be harsh and repulsive. We will be courteous, obliging, kind, and benevolent to everyone.

—Hannah Sinclair: *A Letter to Catherine*

MAY 3

## *The Rest of the World*

While we travel through the wilderness of this world, much of the comfort of our journey depends on good relationships with our fellow travelers. That's why our Savior took special care to unite us in bonds of friendship and love. By his instruction and example, by earnest persuasions and powerful motives, he calms our passions and takes away our rough edges. These things hinder us from joining and cementing together.

If the only people we had to deal with were sincere Christians, we would find it easy to live in harmony and love. There would be few occasions to quarrel. But our Savior knew that we would be a minority in the world. Many would oppose him, and many more would neglect the practice of Christianity. He understood that his followers would meet with much opposition and hatred for their Master's sake. He wanted us to be able to maintain a serene tranquility amid all these storms. He wanted us to be like him and happy in ourselves.

To love those who have obliged us is commonplace. To favor those who have never wronged us is but a piece of ordinary humanity. But our religion requires us to extend kindness even to those who have hurt us, and who continue to do so and wish us mischief. Our religion requires that we never design any other revenge against our most bitter enemies than to wish them well and do them all the good we can. For our Savior said, "Love your enemies" (Luke 6:27).

— Henry Scougal
*The Indispensable Duty of Loving Our Enemies*

MAY 4

## Church Fights

When you observe arguments and troubles in the church, remember that we are frail. Don't be dismayed or depressed. If some people quit, if the whole church seems to be crumbling, remember that God is the foundation of the church. "God's solid foundation stands firm, sealed with this inscription: 'The Lord knows those who are his'" (2 Timothy 2:19). The church is not built on the will of men, but on the goodness and mercy of God.

Although the upper part of the building may be crumbling, God keeps the foundation secure. It will not be shaken. There are many rebels and hypocrites in the world today. Trust God. Never doubt that he will take care of us to the end.

—John Calvin: *The Sure Foundation*

MAY 5

## *True Believers*

One heaven will hold all kinds of people. Why are we broken into factions? Such divisions are the tools of hatred, persecution, and war. They need not be the natural result of differing opinions.

We get into trouble when we make our own religious opinion an article of faith. We want everyone to agree with our point of view. This makes us quarrel and quarrels produce factions. We take sides. We become aggressive "true believers." We think God agrees with us. We think our loving God requires us to hate anyone who disagrees with us. Our personal religion requires us to persecute all other religions.

Enraged, we preserve the body but destroy the soul of religion. In our enthusiasm for correct faith, we forget to love. Consequently, we squander the fruit of both.

—Jeremy Taylor: *The Liberty of Prophesying*

MAY 6

## *Public Prayer*

It is important to engage in public prayer with others assembled together. One place is not holier than another. The whole earth God created is equally holy. But Christ gives us a special promise: "Where two or three come together in my name, there am I with them" (Matthew 18:20). There is no better reason to attend church.

He is not telling us to come together to make music; we come together to pray with others.

—John Knox: *A Treatise on Prayer*


MAY 7

## *Inclusive*

Who has ever heard of a rational person who cares for and clothes one part of his body and leaves the remainder destitute and naked? We naturally take care of all the members of our body.

The Church must do the same: "Now you are the body of Christ, and each one of you is a part of it" (1 Corinthians 12:27). Everyone who is born of God and knows of the Spirit of the Lord is called into one body of love. We are ready by such love to serve our neighbors, not only with money and goods, but also with life and blood in the manner of Christ.

We practice love as much as we are able. We allow no one to be a beggar among us. We receive the miserable, console the afflicted, assist the needy, clothe the naked, feed the hungry, and do not turn our faces from the poor.

—Menno Simons: *Writings*

MAY 8

# *War*

War does not answer international issues. Armies advance toward each other. What are they going to do? They will shoot each other through the head or heart, stab and butcher each other. Why? What harm have they done to one another? Most of them are complete strangers to each other.

A matter is in dispute relative to the mode of taxation. These countrymen, children of the same parents, are ordered to murder each other with all possible haste to prove who is in the right. What an argument! What a method of proof! What an amazing way of deciding controversies! Are there no wise men among us? Is there no one who is able to judge between brothers? Brother going to war against brother is a painful evil among us. We are captives of folly and madness.

—John Wesley: *Address*

MAY 9

## Is Unity Possible?

Different people prefer different religious expression. There is an infinite variety of religious opinion. These differences have caused great divisions and factions among Christians. Some have attempted to correct this situation. Most of them have used poor judgment, like a doctor who mistakenly misapplies an excellent medicine and misses his cure. Attempts at unity have been ineffectual because they put their help in the wrong place. They have tried to cure the symptoms and left the disease alone until it has become almost incurable.

Some have attempted to reunite factions by proposing a universal guide. If everyone could agree on the guide, their thinking would be harmonious. The issue then became the selecting of a proper guide. This process became part of the fire they were trying to extinguish.

Others thought of making unity a law. But even if the entire world agrees with this law, its interpretation remains full of variety. The law becomes a part of the disease they are trying to cure.

—Jeremy Taylor: *The Liberty of Prophesying*


MAY 10

## Church and State

The community is in an uproar and has sounded the alarm. People want to expel a fog of error and heresy with swords and guns, when only light can scatter such fogs and darkness.

It is possible to preach against an established religion without a breach of civil peace. If a breach occurs, it is not the result of doctrine, but of an overexcited and vicious opposition. Such persons break the peace when they cry out for prisons and swords against any who cross their judgment or practice of religion. The sword can make a whole nation of hypocrites. The civil court is not able to help anyone to religious repentance. "Jesus, knowing that they intended to come and make him king by force, withdrew again into the hills by himself" (John 6:15).
—Roger Williams: *The Bloody Tenet of Persecution*


MAY 11

## To the Governor of New York

You have directed us not to receive any of those people called Quakers. Some consider them to be seducers of the people. We can't condemn them in this case, neither can we stretch out our hands against them, to punish, banish, or persecute them.

The law of love, peace and liberty in our states extends to Jews, Turks, and Egyptians, as they are considered children of Adam. Jesus condemns hatred, war, and bondage. We will not offend one of his little ones, whatever name or title they use. Whether they are Presbyterian, Independent, Baptist, or Quaker does not matter. We are glad to see anything of God in any of them, desiring to do unto others as we desire they should do to us.

If any of these people come to us in love, we cannot in conscience lay violent hands upon them, but allow them to move freely. In this we are true subjects both of Church and State. We are bound by law to do good to all and evil to none.

—Edward Hart: *Remonstrance*

MAY 12

## Christian Latitude

Many struggle to find a way to reconcile differences of religious opinion. They recognize that so far nothing has been successful. They believe that as long as there is a variety of thinking, Christ's kingdom is not advanced. Few realize that as long as we have such different ideas and ways of doing things, total unity is not possible. Good Christians have a great variety of education, personalities, hopes, interests, weaknesses, and degrees of understanding. There is no way they will ever be of one mind. What is impossible to do is not necessary to do. It would be easier to stop an earthquake by pressing your shoulder to the ground.

—Jeremy Taylor: *The Liberty of Prophesying*

MAY 13

## Censoriousness

We are very adept at censuring others, but we will not allow ourselves to be corrected. Nothing shows our weakness more than to be so sharp-sighted at spotting the failures of other people while being blind to our own.

When the activities of a neighbor are in the spotlight, we can have our wits about us. We are quick and critical, can split a hair, and spot every failure and infirmity. But we are insensitive and have very little sense of our own failures and infirmities.

We have a right to censure if we have a heart to help. Anything else is cruelty.

—William Penn: *Some Fruits of Solitude*


MAY 14

## Making Amends

If you have injured another, admit your fault rather than defend yourself. It is no honor to maintain what it is dishonorable to do.

We should be quicker to make up with our neighbor than to do him wrong. Instead of being vindictive, we should allow him to determine when he is satisfied. In controversies too often some say, "Both are to blame." Neutrality is an attempt to excuse a lack of concern. Others will say, "They are both alike." This involves the injured with the guilty in order to cover the injustice to the wronged party.

—William Penn: *Some Fruits of Solitude*

MAY 15

## Sharing

Let husband and wife carefully avoid the distinction of mine and yours. This is the basis for all laws, suits, and wars in the world. Let them own things together. What they have serves the necessities of both.

As the heart is placed in the middle of the chest and yet beats more strongly on one side, you can feel its pulse on the other side also. The influence of the heart is equal to all the body. It is the same way with marriage. Some duties may be more one spouse's responsibility, but serve both.

—Jeremy Taylor: *The Marriage Ring*

MAY 16

## Different Kinds

"In a large house there are articles not only of gold and silver, but also of wood and clay; some are for noble purposes and some for ignoble" (2 Timothy 2:20). While there may be furnishings of gold and silver on the dining room table, the kitchen will have rough pots and pans. The finest house has containers for garbage and refuse.

The house of God has a variety of people in its membership. If there are wicked hypocrites in the church of God, it must not bother us. Some of them may actually be highly esteemed. The house of God is a great house. We may wish it were completely pure and that it had no flaws, but that is not the way it is.

Why? Because God assembles a great variety of utensils and vessels. Jesus said, "The kingdom of heaven is like a net that was let down into the lake and caught all kinds of fish. When it was full, the fishermen pulled it up on the shore. Then they sat down and collected the good fish in baskets, but threw the bad away" (Matthew 13:47f).

—John Calvin: *Behavior in the Church*

MAY 17

## *The Right Congregation*

Attend church where you find the warmest sense of religion, where devotion exceeds formality, and practice corresponds with teaching. Try to find a church with at least as much love as zeal. Where you discover such a society, there you will find the Church of God.

A devout man is one thing, a stickler is quite another. To be furious in religion is to be irreligiously religious. It is better to be of no church than to be bitter for any. Some people think they may scold, rail, hate, rob, and kill for the sake of God. But nothing in us that is unlike God can please him. We presume greatly when we send our passions upon God's errands. Zeal with love is good. Without love, it is good for nothing.

—William Penn: *Some Fruits of Solitude*

MAY 18

## *Disagreement*

No Christian is to be put to death, dismembered, or otherwise persecuted for his opinion. Whoever persecutes a disagreeing person arms the entire world against himself and everyone else who agrees with him. Suppose the scales of authority swing in favor of his adversary. Can he beg for mercy for himself and his party when he showed none to others? If he says that he is to be spared because what he believes is true and the one he persecuted was in error, he is ridiculous. Both he and his victim are liable to heresy. Whether either may be true is not for him to judge. One or the other may be in error, but persecution is extremely imprudent. Popular sympathy follows all persons in misery, and that compassion breeds agreement of affections and persuasions. It is counterproductive to attempt to kill an idea.

—Jeremy Taylor: *The Liberty of Prophesying*

MAY 19

## Living with Imperfection

Learn to live with a less than perfect church. Wicked and good people exist together. Some do not want to catch the church in any fault. They depart if they are troubled if the reformation is not complete. They cry out, "Could *this* be the church of God?" They feel defiled and separate themselves from it. They wish they could correct everyone's faults.

By all means, let's not be complacent about evil in the church. We must not allow it to grow and spread. Let's earnestly desire the temple of God to remain pure and clean. Even so, we are required to coexist with grievous evils we are not able to correct. Regardless of the world's influence, do not estrange yourself from the church of God. God may also be working through those who are less than pure. This does not excuse them, but God will find a way to use them that will bring him glory.

—John Calvin: *Behavior in the Church*

MAY 20

## Mixed Grain

When the gospel is preached, many will appear to receive it. For a while everyone will seem to be among the faithful. Some then turn aside and become separated. Jesus compared the church of God to a barn floor where wheat and chaff are mixed. "His winnowing fork is in his hand and he will clear his threshing floor, gathering the wheat into his barn and burning up the chaff with unquenchable fire" (Matthew 3:12).

Our Lord is helping us to understand that during this life the church will never be without mixture. Hypocrites will always be present. Some will assent to the doctrines of faith and they will be assumed to be Christian. They may do well for a while. Then they begin to despise God, using deceit, malice, violence, extortion, and cruelty toward their neighbors. They may grow up in the church, but there will be a division. "All the nations will be gathered before him, and he will separate the people one from another as a shepherd separates the sheep from the goats" (Matthew 25:32).

—John Calvin: *Behavior in the Church*

MAY 21

## *Keeping Family Tensions in Check*

Stifle little things as fast as they appear. If you allow them to survive and increase they cause trouble. A fly bothers some more than an injury. A gnat can disturb sleep. In the frequent little accidents of a family, reason is not always at work. Poorly chosen words can turn a trifling trouble into a violent passion. Add no new provocations to the accident. Do not add fuel to the fire and peace will soon return. Sparks from a flint do not last long.

Be sure to avoid any behavior that irritates another family member. Elephant trainers never appear before the elephants in white. Bull keepers avoid wearing red because they know it will provoke the bulls.

—Jeremy Taylor: *The Marriage Ring*

MAY 22

## *Backhanded Slander*

When the envious attempt to slander another person, they are afraid you will begin to detect their malice. They will assure you that what they have reported "is only the popular opinion." They could never believe "things are as bad as they are said to be." They always hope for the best. They never believe or report ill of anyone. They pass the story on only to do their friend the service "of protecting their disbelief of it." More reputations are hinted away from false friends than are openly destroyed by enemies. An *if* or a *but*, or a mortified look, or an ambiguous shake of the head can be more effective than the whole artillery of malice.

—Hester Chapone: *Envy*

MAY 23

## *Women Preachers*

We should be careful when making rules for church government. As unseemly as it may appear today for a woman to preach, it should be remembered that nothing is impossible with God. Why do we think it is impossible or improper for a woman to preach? The Savior died for women as well as men.

Mary was the first to preach the risen Savior. The resurrection is the central core of Christianity. Some will say that Mary did not expound the Scripture, therefore, she did not actually preach. Preaching then was a great deal simpler. If it were not, the unlearned fishermen could not have preached the gospel at all.

In my wanderings, preaching according to my ability, I have frequently found families who told me that they had not for several years been to a meeting. And yet, while listening to hear what God would say by this poor colored female instrument, they have believed with trembling and tears. I firmly believe I have sown seed in the name of the Lord.

—Jarena Lee: *Life and Religious Experience*

MAY 24

## *Unity*

The eternal Spirit of God is one and not divisive. "Every kingdom divided against itself will be ruined, and every city or household divided against itself will not stand" (Matthew 12:25). Notice your own situation. If you are divided, you cannot stand. I speak in love and tenderness to your soul. Keep in the light, which is one, and in the power, which is one, and in the measure of life revealed in you, which is one. There is no division here. Instead of separation, there is gathering and knitting. If you love the light, then come to the light to be tested.

—Margaret Fell Fox
*A General Epistle to Friends, 1655*

MAY 25

## *Stress and Bickering*

A little difficulty can put a strain on a marriage. Trouble with children can cause quarreling and discontent between the parents. Stress can create strife in the family. Many people simply come to accept this as a fact of life.

A husband and wife could try this: Go off somewhere and humble your souls before God. Go into your bedroom and admit that some of your problems are of your own making. The cloud will dissipate. The sun will shine again.

—Jeremiah Burroughs
*Rare Jewel of Christian Contentment*

MAY 26

## *Primary Motive*

Never marry except for love, and love only what is lovely. If love is not your primary motive, you will soon grow weary of marriage and stray from your promise.

The difference between lust and love is that lust is volatile and love is steady. Love grows; lust wastes. The reason for this is that one springs from a union of souls, and the other from a union of the senses.
—William Penn: *Some Fruits of Solitude*

MAY 27

## Children and Parents in the Lord

Be grateful to your parents. You owe them a lot. There was a time when you were totally dependent upon their kindness. You were not able to take care of yourself. If a parent's arm had not supported you, you would have perished. You were a burden and a bother and there was no way you could repay their affection.

Did your parents forsake you? How many sleepless nights did your cries disturb? They tenderly watched over you when you were sick. They watched with pleasure as you grew up to your present state. What do you possess that you did not receive from them? God is your great parent and best friend. Every good comes from God. But God is pleased to give you everything through the kindness of your parents.

When you think how often you have forfeited all this kindness, and how ready your parents have been to forgive you and continue their favors, be filled with tender gratitude. There is no greater monster than an unthankful child who thinks that they have done nothing for him because they have not done all he desires.

—William Ellery Channing: *The Duties of Children*

MAY 28

## *Nothing New*

The whole body of the Church has always been, and to the end will be, troubled by the wicked. There is nothing new about what goes on in churches. St. Paul asks if we should not expect and endure "trouble or hardship or persecution or famine or nakedness or danger of sword? As it is written: 'For your sake we face death all day long; we are considered as sheep to be slaughtered'" (Romans 8:35f).

Therefore, when you see how the Church of God is trampled on today by the secular community, how one barks and another bites, how they torture, how they plot against her, remember that the same thing was done long ago. Sometimes God gives the Church a truce and time of refreshment. But God still allows his Church to battle as long as it is in this world. "When we are cursed, we bless; when we are persecuted, we endure it; when we are slandered, we answer kindly" (1 Corinthians 4:12). Take courage. Our predecessors were as frail as we are, and they endured victoriously.

—John Calvin: *Enduring Persecution for Christ*

MAY 29

## Church at Home

Paul sends a greeting to "the church that meets at their house" (Romans 16:5). There is nothing absurd about a church in a house. Perhaps there was a congregation of Christians who met there at stated times. On the other hand, the church in that house may have simply been a religious, well-governed family that kept up the worship of God. When the power of religion controls a family, it will turn such a house into a church.

—Matthew Henry: *Commentary on the Whole Bible*


MAY 30

## Marriage

Marriage is a school of virtue. If being single allows more privacy of devotion, marriage is an exercise of more graces. It has more care, but less danger. It is fuller of sorrow, and fuller of joy. Marriage lies under more burdens, but it is supported by all the strengths of love.

—Jeremy Taylor: *The Marriage Ring*


MAY 31

## Let God Judge

Be hesitant to judge or condemn another person. Love is not quickly offended.

To be sure, the world is full of offenses and easily offended. If our Savior returned to earth and spoke with a woman at the well as he once did, there would be some who would be offended by his behavior. Both of them would disturb us.

Don't be rash in passing judgment. It is a mistake to judge a person too quickly without full knowledge. The rule is to seek your neighbor's good rather than your own.

Why does God allow such offenses in the world? We don't know. "How unsearchable his judgments, and his paths beyond tracing out" (Romans 11:33). But we know God can use them to accomplish good.

—Hugh Latimer: *Fruitful Sermons*

## JUNE
*Faith*

JUNE 1

## *The Jewel of Faith*

God's grace is of infinite value. Faith is a jewel. It is correct to call it "a faith as precious as ours" (2 Peter 1:1). What is love but a divine sparkle in the soul? A soul that is decorated with grace is like a room that is richly hung with tapestries, or the night sky illumined with glittering stars. These are the true riches. They are all that is necessary to make the soul content.

Augustine observed that earthly riches are full of poverty. They are not able to enrich the soul. A threadbare soul is often under silk clothes. Moreover, earthly riches decay. You cannot take gold and silver with you to heaven. A believer is rich toward God. The Lord has given you something much better than the treasures of this world. He gives you the jewel. Does it matter if he does not give you the box? We have God's fullness and do not complain of the world's emptiness. "LORD, you have assigned me my portion and my cup; you have made my lot secure" (Psalm 16:5).

—Thomas Watson
*The Art of Divine Contentment*


JUNE 2

## *Freely Given*

Faith is a gift of God. Some pretend to have faith and consider themselves to be believers. Their manner of living contradicts this. True faith purifies the heart (Acts 15:9). It overcomes the world (1 John 5:4). "The only thing that counts is faith expressing itself through love" (Galatians 5:6). Anything less than true faith will not produce these results. It is an imitation faith.

—Hannah Sinclair: *A Letter to Catherine*

JUNE 3

## *The Object of Faith*

Don't imagine that Christian faith is bare knowledge of God, or an understanding of Scripture that flutters in the brain without touching the heart. Faith is a firm, solid confidence in the mercy of God as the gospel promises. The substance of that promise defines faith. Faith rests so much on this foundation that it cannot stand without it.

When we receive the mercy the Lord presents to us through the promise of the gospel, we accept his word through faith. "Faith is being sure of what we hope for and certain of what we do not see" (Hebrews 11:1). All the promises of God center on Christ. He is the confirmation of the promises. Christ, then, is the object of faith. In him, faith contemplates all the riches of divine mercy.

—John Calvin: *Instruction in Faith*

JUNE 4

## Cheap Faith

It does not make sense to pretend to have faith if it bears no fruit. "Suppose a brother or sister is without clothes and daily food. If one of you says to him, 'Go, I wish you well; keep warm and well fed,' but does nothing about his physical needs, what good is it?" (James 2:15f). How can a charity that consists in bare words help either you or the poor? Will you come before God with such an empty show of charity? "Faith by itself, if it is not accompanied by action, is dead" (James 2:17). We think that a bare profession of faith will save us. It is a cheap and easy religion that says, "We believe the articles of the Christian faith." We are deluded if we think this is enough to bring us to heaven. A mock-faith is as detestable as mock-charity.

—Matthew Henry
*Commentary on the Whole Bible*

JUNE 5

## The Heart of Religion

Religion is a reverence for God and a demonstration of that in good works. Faith is at the root of both. Without faith we cannot please God and neither can we respect what we do not believe.

—William Penn: *Some Fruits of Solitude*

## JUNE 6

## Faith and Reason

Clearly defined knowledge is mainly of things we can see. We more easily form definite conceptions of objects we can handle than of objects belonging to the inner sense. There is no difficulty in studying what we can see, hear and touch.

We naturally become most adept with the materials of our main occupation. One trained as a physicist accurately perceives even subtle physical forces. A logician has a strong grasp on logical distinctions. They may both be adrift at sea when it comes to catching the imaginative and emotional aspects of things. A person who is strong in a special field may be weak in other regions.

When scientific and logical minds turn toward the spiritual world, the objects there seem vaporous. When we think of God and the soul's relation to him, we feel as if we had stepped into a world in which human understanding can find little firm footing. We cannot adequately express such truths. We crave a more exact outline. We are tempted to reject as nonexistent things which are not subject to familiar rules. We try to limit the orb of belief to the orb of exact knowledge. Spiritual realities are offensive to such a mind.

—John Shairp
*Hindrances to Spiritual Growth*

JUNE 7
## *Prayer and Faith*
Prayer is the nurse of faith. The way to build up ourselves in our most holy faith is to continue in prayer. Our prayers will become more effective and our faith more fervent. This is praying in the Holy Spirit, whether it is done with or without a prescribed form.

—Matthew Henry
*Commentary on the Whole Bible*

JUNE 8
## *Living Faith*
Do not be deceived. The faith that does not produce repentance, love, and good works is not living faith. True faith cleanses the human heart of pride, anger, desire and everything ugly. Faith fills us with a love for God and others that "is as strong as death" (Song of Songs 8:6). It is a love that works for God, a love that is glad to "spend and be spent" (2 Corinthians 12:15 KJV), that joyfully endures every difficulty. Such faith is not almost, but altogether, Christian.

—John Wesley: *The Almost Christian*

JUNE 9
## *Eye of the Soul*
"Faith is being sure of what we hope for and certain of what we do not see" (Hebrews 11:1). Faith demonstrates

to the eye of the mind the reality of those things that cannot be discerned by the body's eye. Faith is the firm assent of the soul to the divine revelation. It helps the soul to apply itself to worthy affections and activities. Faith serves the believer instead of sight. Faith is to the soul as all the senses are to the body. If faith does not reveal invisible things to the soul and excite the soul to take action, it is nothing more than an opinion or fancy.
—Matthew Henry: *Commentary on the Whole Bible*

JUNE 10

## *Personal Faith*

To agree with the belief of a master in theology or simply to accept what a church teaches does not give sufficient reason for our faith. We stand on our own foundation, not theirs. Their answers will not be accepted as our own in the Day of Judgment.

We have a right of private judgment. If we give it up, we let go of our capacity for faith. We undermine the foundation of personal religion and can no longer live in the rational exercise of faith or hope. Have no confidence in human authority. Religious instructors are forbidden to have dominion over the faith of others.
—Aaron Bancroft: *Sermons*

## JUNE 11
## *Applied Faith*

An individual may have deep convictions, ecstatic emotions, and fiery zeal without a heart that is right with God. It is easy to say, "Lord, Lord" (Matthew 7:21). We can avow our belief in the doctrines of the Word made flesh. We can attach ourselves to some division of the great Christian army and swear allegiance to its flag. But to fight the good fight of faith, to demonstrate the reality of our love by our actions, to embody the doctrines of religion in a life of holiness—this is no easy task. Yet it is indispensable.

—George Junkin: *Truth and Freedom*

## JUNE 12
## *Faith's Purpose*

Christian faith lays the foundation for a worship that is both rational and affectionate. The light of understanding concurs with the devotion of the heart. The most profound reverence is united with the most cordial love.

Christian faith is not a system of speculative truths. It is not simply a lesson of moral instruction. By a train of high discoveries that it reveals, it elevates the mind and purifies the affections. By the assistance of devotion, faith encourages virtue.

—Hugh Blair: *The Hour and the Event of all Time*

JUNE 13

## A Gift of God

If we honestly consider how blind we are to God's heavenly secrets, we will understand that faith is a unique and precious gift of God. "For what human being knows what is truly human except the human spirit that is within? So also no one comprehends what is truly God's except the Spirit of God" (1 Corinthians 2:11 NRSV). If the truth of God in us wavers even in things we can see with our eyes, how will it be firm and stable where the Lord promises things we cannot see or understand?

Faith is a light of the Holy Spirit that enlightens our understanding. Christ has "put his Spirit in our hearts as a deposit, guaranteeing what is to come" (2 Corinthians 1:22). The Spirit witnesses to our spirit that God is our Father. "The Spirit himself testifies with our spirit that we are God's children" (Romans 8:16).

—John Calvin: *Instruction in Faith*


JUNE 14

## Not Equally Important

Don't be concerned about the trivial details of faith. Faith is not a collection of opinions. People who dispute the fine points of religion are frequently the least acquainted with God. If your faith is nothing but firmly held opinions, you will be loud and obnoxious.

If your faith rests in the knowledge and love of God, you will be diplomatic and attractive.

It is not often possible to improve on a well-known truth. Don't give too much attention to disputes that have little to do with spiritual health. When hypocrites are trying to feed on husks and shells, offer them some of God's joys. You do not need to defend all of God's truths. Concentrate on the important things. The least controversial issues are the most valuable for faith.
—Richard Baxter: *The Saints' Everlasting Rest*

JUNE 15
## *Fruitful Faith*
A faithful person is a fruitful person. Faith produces results. "Walk in the footsteps of the faith that our father Abraham had" (Romans 4:12). Faith allowed Abraham to perform every duty that God required of him. Faith is the force behind every Christian act. Prayer is an act of faith. Obedience is an act of faith. The Christian actually lives by faith.
—Thomas Hooker: *The Activity of Faith*

JUNE 16
## *Faith and Courage*
Someone may urge us to suffer for the name of Christ. Suffering will have no effect unless we are sure of the

cause for which we fight. When someone asks us to risk our lives, it is absolutely necessary to know on what grounds; the risk requires the certainty of faith. Some may foolishly expose themselves to great hazards, keeping an absurd opinion and dream. Such impetuosity is more frenzy than Christian zeal. There is no sound judgment in those who toss their lives away for worthless causes. No call to suffer persecution for the gospel will impress us if no true certainty of faith is imprinted in our hearts. To risk life upon a "perhaps" is rashness rather than Christian courage.

—John Calvin: *Enduring Persecution for Christ*

JUNE 17

## *Hand in Hand*

There are those who teach that St. Paul spoke against the dignity of faith when he said, "These three remain: faith, hope and love. But the greatest of these is love" (1 Corinthians 13:13). We must understand that St. Paul is not speaking here of the justifying faith that brings everlasting life. He means the faith that produces miracles such as moving mountains. He is not referring to living faith in Christ. Such a faith is rich in love. Love flows from this faith.

Love is a child of faith. You can't really love unless you believe. Faith and love are inseparable. Take no offense in the fact that Scripture commends love so highly. He that commends the daughter commends the

# FAITH 123

mother also. Love is the daughter. Faith is the mother. Where faith is, there is love.

—Hugh Latimer: *On Christian Love*

JUNE 18

## Overly Eager

Wrestling with hard questions on the edge of human knowledge has a wonderful fascination to young and ardent spirtis. They leap without fear into the abyss. They expect to dive down to depths deeper than anyone else has ever gone. They expect to solve problems that have baffled the world's best thinkers. I have seen too many young people, some of them the finest spirits of our time, setting forth with too much confidence in their own ability. They imagine they will be able to meet all difficulties. Soon enough, they crash.

—John Shairp: *Hindrances to Spiritual Growth*

JUNE 19

## Faith of Demons

Bare speculation and knowledge are the faith of devils. "You believe that there is one God. Good! Even the demons believe that—and shudder" (James 2:19). Yes, it is better to believe in God than to be an atheist. Yes, it is good that you do not worship idols and believe that there is only one God. But to stop here, and have a good opinion of yourself and your view of God, is not nearly enough. If you are content with a bare assent to articles of faith, and some speculation on them, remember that even the demons do that. As their faith and knowledge only serve to excite horror, so in a little time will yours. To recite our creed, "I believe in God the Father Almighty," will not ultimately distinguish us from demons. We need to give ourselves to God, and love him, and delight ourselves in him, and serve him. The demons can't do that.

—Matthew Henry
*Commentary on the Whole Bible*


JUNE 20
## *In Faith*
"Examine yourselves to see whether you are in the faith" (2 Corinthians 13:5). The apostle does not ask whether or not the faith is in you. He asks the reverse. Are you in the faith? Alcohol controls someone who is drunk. A person who is in love is motivated by that love. If you are in the faith, then you are under the command of faith. When you pray, faith composes your prayer. When you obey God, faith is at work. If you live, it is faith that enlivens your soul. Faith accomplishes wonderful things in the soul of the believer. Faith never rests. It is always at work and it inspires valuable activity. Faith will move your tongue to speak.

—Thomas Hooker: *The Activity of Faith*

JUNE 21

## *Faith is for Now*

"Now we see but a poor reflection; then we shall see face to face. Now I know in part; then I shall know fully, even as I am fully known" (1 Corinthians 13:12). Faith is as puzzling as a mirror. Only the image, not the actual face, is in the glass. Faith does not give us the radiant countenance of eternal Deity, but a mere image of him, an image received through the Word. As a riddle points to something more than it expresses, so faith suggests something clearer than what it perceives. In the life to come, mirror and riddle, faith and its demonstration, will stop. God's face and our own will be revealed clearly. We will know God then as well as God knows us now.

—Martin Luther: *Sermon on Christian Love*

JUNE 22

## *Equal Quality*

"To those who through the righteousness of our God and Savior Jesus Christ have received a faith as precious as ours" (2 Peter 1:1). The apostle Peter says every Christian participates in the same precious faith as the great saints. If a person has only one gold coin, the gold in it is as good as the gold in a million dollars. It is made of the same metal. So it is with faith.

Or consider grafting trees. Many scions of the same kind may be grafted into one stock. They all participate equally in the strength of the stock. The Lord Jesus Christ is the stock, as it were, into which all the faithful are grafted by faith. The fruit is the same on each limb. There may be differences in size, but the fruit has the same nature. A little apple has the same taste as a great one on the same tree. Every faithful Christian has the same holiness of heart and life. One Christian's fruit may be poor and small in comparison with others, but it is the same kind of fruit.

—Thomas Hooker: *The Activity of Faith*

JUNE 23

## *Faith's Awareness*

Faith has the same place in the devotional life that our senses have in the natural world. Faith is actually another kind of sense, an awareness of spiritual things. Faith extends itself into God's truth. Because our Lord is the principal object of our faith, we may call it "faith in Jesus Christ."

—Henry Scougal
*The Life of God in the Soul of Man*

JUNE 24

## *Great Faith*

Our Lord calls the centurion's faith "great" even though it rose no higher than to prompt him to affirm, "Say the word, and my servant will be healed" (Matthew 8:8). A similar case can be seen in the

Canaanite woman who asked Jesus for help. He seemed at first to rebuff her, but she persisted. "Even the dogs eat the crumbs that fall from their masters' table" (Matthew 15:27). Our Savior's response is a comfort to every discouraged sinner. "Woman, you have great faith!" (Matthew 15:28).

Faith is like a sundial which is of little service unless the sun shines upon it. The Holy Spirit must illumine our faith.

—Augustus Toplady: *Complete Works*

JUNE 25

## *The Work of Faith*

Faith is more than having a precise understanding of doctrine. It is an uplifting principle. While faith may clarify thinking, its true function is to become a vital part of our living. It directs our desire as well as it improves our knowledge. It changes our attitude and preferences. Faith gives us a new heart, a new life.

—Hannah More: *Practical Piety*

JUNE 26

## *General Faith*

Love inevitably accompanies true Christian faith. There is a general faith in God that is loveless. This faith is also a gift. Such things as the gift of tongues, the gift of knowledge, or the gift of prophecy may be

found in people who are less than Christian. It is possible that even Judas performed miracles. This general faith is powerless to justify or to cleanse. It does not bring about change in the individual who has it. It leaves a person as unaltered as do the gifts of intellect, health, eloquence and riches.
—Martin Luther: *Sermon on Christian Love*

JUNE 27

## *Increasing Faith*

The apostles were prime ministers of state in Christ's kingdom, yet they admitted their faith was deficient. They saw the need to improve it. "The apostles said to the Lord, 'Increase our faith!'" (Luke 17:5). They wanted the discoveries of faith to be clearer, the desires of faith to be stronger, the dependences of faith to be more firm and fixed, the dedications of faith more unwavering, and the delights of faith more pleasing.

Earnestly desire an increase of faith. Offer that desire to God in prayer.
—Matthew Henry: *Commentary on the Whole Bible*

JUNE 28

## *Faith Now*

"According to your faith will it be done to you" (Matthew 9:29). Christ assures us that as our faith is, so it shall be done. This is why we fall short of salvation in Christ. We do not desire it. Many only want their faith to help them into heaven when they die. This is not the same as wanting Christ to be your Savior. If Christ saves you it must be done in this life, by changing everything about you. Faith results in a new way of thinking and behaving. The change is as radical as when the blind see, the lame walk, and the mute speak. Being saved is being made like Jesus. We gain his humility, meekness, and self-denial. We inherit his love of God, his desire of doing God's will, and seeking only God's honor.

—William Law: *Mystical Writings*

JUNE 29

## Faith Comes to Your World

Everything Christ says ultimately concerns faith. He speaks of nothing else than of faith. Faith is the basis of everything. If you have faith, you will always do what is good. Without faith you will fall into sin.

Christ commanded his disciples to preach the gospel to the entire world. Wise men call a human a little world, a microcosm. Then preach to yourself, O man, woman, and child. The world is in you also. Preach to your knowledge. Say to it, "If you draw near this truth, you will have much faith." Preach to your will. Say, "You see that everything passes away. Therefore, do not love the world, love Christ." To your memory say, "Be thankful for the mercies God has shown you." To your imagination proclaim, "Set nothing before my eyes but the crucified one. Embrace him."

Then go through all the cities of your world and preach to them. Say to your eyes, "Do not look at vanity." To your ears say, "Listen only to the words of Jesus." To your tongue say, "Speak no more evil." Your tongue is a giant rock that rolls from the summit of a mountain. At first it falls slowly, then ever faster and more furiously. It begins with gentle murmuring and ends with open blasphemy. To your palate say, "Do a little penance. Keep your senses clean." To your hands say, "Do good and give alms."

—Girolamo Savonarola: *The Ascension of Christ*

JUNE 30

## *Higher Ground*

The correct way for a renewed heart to move is upward. True faith aspires to higher things. It reaches toward its origin in heaven. With deep roots, it stretches high. Well nourished, it is always able to grow some more. You may recognize genuine goodness by its constant attempt to be better. None of the virtues is ever complete. Regardless of the spiritual stage you have reached, there is no satisfaction, no willingness to stop at that level. No Christian grace is ever finished. We can always carry it higher.

—Hannah More: *Practical Piety*

# JULY
## *Patience and Contentment*

## JULY 1

## *The Ambition of Immortal Spirits*

Have you ever sat down to the full enjoyment of the present, without a hope or a wish unsatisfied? Did you have no thought for the future, no longing for some remote or inaccessible object? The present is but a moment of time. The instant we call it our own, it abandons us. It is not the actual sensations that occupy the mind. It is what is to come next. We live in the future. We are interested in our vision of tomorrow not the reality of today. When tomorrow comes, the animating hope becomes dull reality.

We must have something to look forward to. The mere possession of wealth and its pleasures will not be enough to satisfy. Our spirits are restless. Nothing in this world will ever fill up our capacity for happiness. We are born for something beyond time. Only religion can accommodate this property of our nature.

—Thomas Chalmers
*The Restlessness of Human Ambition*


## JULY 2

## *Why?*

Discontent is commonplace. A lack of contentment is as troubling to the soul as a disease is to the body. Discontent can be a spiritual handicap, And there is no excuse for it even if it occurs naturally.

There is no more beautiful Christian ornament than contentment. If we are going to enjoy life in this world, contentment is the key.

Why do we lack contentment? "Why are you downcast, O my soul? Why so disturbed within me?" (Psalm 42:11). Of all God's creatures, we have the least reason to be discontented. Do we deserve anything from God? Does God owe us anything?

If this fretting leprosy infects you, you are probably setting yourself above God. You think you are wiser than God. You are trying to tell God what is best for you. Discontent is a devil that can make your heart a little hell. While there may never be perfect contentment in this life, we can begin to tune our instrument here before we play it exactly right in heaven.

—Thomas Watson
*The Art of Divine Contentment*

JULY 3

## *Never Never Land*

There is nothing more effective for quieting a Christian soul than seeking your responsibilities in the circumstances you are now in, and considering your thoughts about being in other conditions a mere temptation.

It is folly to think you would be more content if you could be somewhere else. Children climb a hill and see a higher one at a distance. They think that if they could only be on top of that mountain they could touch the clouds with their fingers. If they should climb such a mountain, they would discover that they are as far from the clouds as they were before. It is the same way with anyone who thinks another circumstance will bring more happiness.

—Jeremiah Burroughs
*Rare Jewel of Christian Contentment*

JULY 4

## *Holy Complaining*

We may cry out to God when we have difficulties. "I pour out my complaint before him; before him I tell my trouble" (Psalm 142:2). It is natural for a child to complain to its father. When our spirits are under pressure, prayer is a safety valve. It eases the heart. Hannah was greatly upset. She said, "I am a woman who is deeply troubled" (1 Samuel 1:15). After she prayed and wept, she was no longer sad.

There is a difference between a holy complaint and a discontented complaint. In the first we complain *to* God. In the other we complain *about* God. Such murmuring is scum that boils off a discontented heart.

—Thomas Watson
*The Art of Divine Contentment*

JULY 5

## *Anywhere Else*

Things look better from a distance. A field of weeds is a delight to the eye when it is far away. A little village can look like a beautiful paradise when seen from a mountaintop, in spite of the trash that is at every door, and the angry brawling of the men and women who live there. Distance softens edges.

On a sunny day, have you ever wished you could go to some distant and more beautiful part of the landscape? Did you think that the people who live there are happier? Did you wish you could quietly wander in some distant grove and forget the distractions of the world? Was there a desire in you to be someplace other than where you were? Instead of enjoying your present situation, you wanted to travel. "Oh, that I had the wings of a dove! I would fly away and be at rest" (Psalm 55:6).

If you ever reached that distant place, rest would remain far from you. The enchantment would gradually melt away, the illusion entirely dissipated. You would be distressed to find that you have carried the same principle of restlessness and discontent along with you.

—Thomas Chalmers
*The Restlessness of Human Ambition*

## JULY 6

## *A Pilgrimage*

When we are at home, rain pouring into the house is an intolerable hardship. But when we are traveling, we are not as concerned about rain and storms. When we are at sea, though we may not have as many things as we keep at home, inconveniences simply do not bother us. Sailors don't care about their clothes when they are on a voyage. They are often dirty and covered with tar. They wear rags. Silk stockings, suits, and laced cuffs will have to wait until they get home. The same is true with food. For now, they make do with salt meat and a little hard crust of bread. That is the way it is at sea and they do not complain.

This is also the way we should be in the world. The truth is, we are in this world like seafarers, tossed by the waves. We are travelers here. Our home is a distant place in another world. "I urge you, as aliens and strangers in the world, to abstain from sinful desires, which war against your soul" (1 Peter 2:11). We are pilgrims and strangers. Do not attempt to satisfy yourself here.

—Jeremiah Burroughs
*Rare Jewel of Christian Contentment*

JULY 7

## Peaceable Prayer

Pray every day. Have no doubt that God hears all your requests. Don't pray like a fretful child. We dishonor God when we angrily complain about what is going on in our lives. Protesting to God that we have not received what we wish is a poor prayer. We defy God in the manner of one who complains to another member of the family, "You don't care about me!" It would be better not to pray at all than to approach God with anger and rage.

Learn to pray with a peaceable heart. St. Paul encourages us to make thanksgiving an important part of our prayers. If we do not immediately receive what we desire, wait patiently. Be satisfied until God is ready to act on your behalf.

—John Calvin: *The Privilege of Prayer*

JULY 8

## What is Best

"Be content with what you have, because God has said, 'Never will I leave you; never will I forsake you'" (Hebrews 13:5). That's an order. It is a royal fiat we are expected to obey. Do not be more restless than the raging sea our Lord ordered to be still. "'You of little faith, why are you so afraid?' Then he got up and rebuked the winds and the waves, and it was completely calm" (Matthew 8:25f).

God's wisdom controls the conditions of our lives. If it is better for us to have a lot, we will have much. If it is better for us to do without, we will lack. God understands that the same condition is not best for everyone. Something that is good for one person may be harmful for another. Sunshine will help one and rain will help another. One condition of life will not fit everyone any more than one suit of clothing will fit every body. Neither prosperity nor adversity is suitable for everyone.

—Thomas Watson: *The Art of Divine Contentment*

JULY 9

## *Faith Cures Discontent*

"We know that in all things God works for the good of those who love him, who have been called according to his purpose" (Romans 8:28). Faith silences grumbling. It inspires satisfaction and resignation. It is a strong support in every misfortune a believer can experience.

Are you sick? You will wait patiently for the day when pain and sorrow will be a thing of the past.

Are you poor and oppressed? Ponder the treasure you have in heaven.

Have you lost a friend? Look forward to the time when you will be among saints and angels.

"We do not lose heart. Though outwardly we are wasting away, yet inwardly we are being renewed day by day. For our light and momentary troubles are achieving for us an eternal glory that far outweighs them all" (2 Corinthians 4:16–17).

—Hannah Sinclair: *A Letter to Catherine*

JULY 10

## *Spiritual Victory*

By contentment a Christian gets a victory over himself. The noblest conquest of all is to rule your own spirit. Passion is a sign of weakness; it is easy to become emotional. To be content in any condition of life is challenging. It is a holy valor deliverable only by the Holy Spirit. To be calm and patient in a changing and dangerous world is worthy of a garland of honor.

Poor Job lost everything. He is one of the most pitiful examples in the Bible. And yet, Job "fell to the ground in worship" (Job 1:20). We would expect him to fall to the ground and curse. He got victory over himself. It is nothing great when someone gives in to passionate emotion, but to be content while denying yourself is sacred.

—Thomas Watson
*The Art of Divine Contentment*

JULY 11

## *Patience under Duress*

I know that God often brings things to pass by contrary means.

My cousin, Russell, wrote me a letter to let me know my husband was offended with me and was taking legal action against me. "Many are those who are my vigorous enemies; those who hate me without reason are numerous. Those who repay my good with evil slander me when I seek what is good" (Psalm 38:19f). I am resolved to take it all patiently, casting all my care on God.

—Anne Clifford: *Diary*


JULY 12

## *Complaining Permitted*

The attainment of true happiness would not take a lot of practice if it were as easy as keeping quiet and not showing our feelings. You can do that with a lot less skill than the apostle Paul had learned. There is more to it than using common gifts and ordinary reasoning.

Actually, there is nothing wrong with protesting to God and complaining to friends. Perhaps we ought to be silent when God is correcting our behavior, but it is not required. It is not a breach of Christian contentment to express how we feel, as long as we do so without screaming and loss of control. "You ought to be quiet and not do anything rash" (Acts 19:36). We can tell our friends the details of how God is dealing with us. Perhaps they may speak a word of encouragement to a weary soul. We might even receive some help to get out of our unpleasant circumstances.

—Jeremiah Burroughs
*Rare Jewel of Christian Contentment*

JULY 13

## *Our Toys*

We are frequently disappointed. The child whines for a toy. The moment he possesses it, he throws it aside and cries for another. When the toys are piled up in heaps around him, he looks at them without pleasure and leaves them without regret. The only good they could yield lay in expectation. The desire for more increases faster than the multiplication of toys. The child is unhappy at last for the same reason as at first—his wishes are ungratified. Still indulging them, and still believing that the gratification of them will furnish the desired enjoyment, he continues to ask for more, only to remain unhappy.

Adults are merely taller children. Honor, wealth, and splendor are the toys on our wish list. However much we accumulate, we remain disappointed and unhappy. God never intended that intelligent beings should be satisfied with these enjoyments.

Moderated desire can accept all the good this world can yield. If you're prepared, you can be content in any situation. You can learn the science of being happy. This ability is an alchemic stone that has the power to change every base metal into gold. You will smile sitting on a stump while Alexander weeps on the throne of the world.

—Timothy Dwight: *The Sovereignty of God*

JULY 14

## *Enjoying it All*

A devoted person will find pleasure in everything God's providence allows. The divine goodness in every experience will be visible. Each event will be a token of love sent by one's dearest Lord and Maker. Unpleasant chastisements lose their sting. One would rejoice that though God did not satisfy the will of a foolish creature, he yet fulfilled his own will and accomplished his own designs—which are infinitely more holy and wise.

—Henry Scougal
*The Life of God in the Soul of Man*

JULY 15

## *Patience on Trial*

Sometimes a faithful person must cope with the criticism and slurs of others. Patience protects us from such things. Try to forgive every wrong directed against you. "Love your enemies, do good to those who hate you, bless those who curse you, pray for those who mistreat you" (Luke 6:27f). How do you pray for them? Ask God to guide them into a better way.

The only way you can show your spiritual strength is to be at peace when you are troubled. It is easy to appear to be patient when you are not being tested.

—John Wycliffe: *The Poor Caitiff*

JULY 16

## *Beyond Reason*

Something the secular world will never understand is the melting of a Christian's will into the will of God. It is not a matter of having our own desires satisfied, but of being in harmony with God's desires. This way we can be satisfied even if we do not receive everything we want.

This is a degree higher than merely submitting to the will of God. A devout Christian embodies the will of God. We can get beyond merely accepting our circumstances. God's will and our will can be identical. We are joined to the Lord in one spirit. What God wants is what we want. We will not only yield to it, we will fervently desire it. If God's will is satisfied, then I am satisfied. "He chose our inheritance for us" (Psalm 47:4).

Until you understand these things, and practice them, you will be a bungler in this business of Christianity.
—Jeremiah Burroughs
*Rare Jewel of Christian Contentment*

JULY 17

## *Spiritual Combat*

"Endure hardship like a good soldier of Christ Jesus" (2 Timothy 2:3). A soldier has a rough time of it. His crude quarters are not as comfortable as his bedroom at home. He understands these conditions are acceptable for a soldier. It would be unseemly for a solder to go whining up and down with his finger in his eye, complaining that he does not have hot meat at every meal, and his bed warmed as it was at home.

Christians are in combat. They are fighting a war with the enemies of their souls. They must be willing to endure hardship. Eventually they will triumph with Jesus Christ. Rough it for now. The traveler spending a night in an inn does not envy its cabinet full of dishes. Why? Because the trip isn't over. The traveler will soon depart. Let's not be troubled when we see others with great wealth. We are going elsewhere. We are only lodging here for the night. It is madness to be frustrated because we do not possess everything we see here. We may be moving on in a quarter of an hour.

—Jeremiah Burroughs
*Rare Jewel of Christian Contentment*

## JULY 18
## *Partially Done*

The discontented person performs religious duties by halves. "Ephraim is a flat cake not turned over" (Hosea 7:8). He is half-baked. He gives God the outside, but not the spiritual part. His soul is not on duty. He gives God only the skin of worship and is perplexed when he receives little more than the shell of comfort.

—Thomas Watson
*The Art of Divine Contentment*

## JULY 19
## *Patience in Prayer*

Be careful not to impose any conditions on how God may answer your prayer. Do not attempt to confine or limit God's merciful activity. Before making any prayer for ourselves, above all things, ask that his will be done. If we are willing to accept the good pleasure of divine providence, we will learn to continue in prayer and wait patiently upon the Lord.

Though God does not show himself to us, he is present with us. God hears our prayers. If, after waiting a long time we don't see any results of our prayer, our faith will give us confidence. God is patient. Ultimately, his will prevails.

—John Calvin: *Instruction in Faith*

JULY 20

## *Petty Envy*

"There are three things that are never satisfied, four that never say, 'Enough!': the grave, the barren womb, land, which is never satisfied with water, and fire" (Proverbs 30:15–16). There is also a fifth insatiable thing: the heart of an envious person.

Trifles bother many. Someone else has a better dress, a more valuable jewel, a newer fashion. Nero was not satisfied to control an empire. Musicians who had more skill than he possessed disturbed him. We pine away because we lack things that are not suitable for us. We complain as if God has dealt harshly with us. We list the things we lack. Our greatest lack is a gratified spirit.

—Thomas Watson
*The Art of Divine Contentment*

JULY 21

## *Delayed Response*

Sometimes God waits a long time before answering our prayers. God is not asleep nor absent from us. Waiting is a time of testing, which also makes us even more joyful when the long awaited expectation finally arrives. Never doubt God's mercy.

If God prolongs your wait to the point that you think he has rejected you, do not stop praying. Let God act in his own good time. Hannah, Sarah, and

Elizabeth greatly desired a baby. After it seemed impossible, their prayers were answered.
—John Knox: *A Treatise on Prayer*

JULY 22

## *Metamorphosis*

Instead of trying to have your problem removed, try to change it. The way you respond to an affliction can metamorphose it. Yes, it will remain, but its effect will be different. You will use it in another way. Instead of asking that it be gone, think, "God has taught me a way to be content though the affliction itself continues." There is a power of grace to turn an affliction into good. The right attitude can take the string and poison out of it. Instead of a natural evil, it becomes a spiritual benefit.

Ambrose said, "Poverty itself is riches to the holy." Luther makes a similar comment in his commentary on Galatians. "A Christian can create joy out of heaviness, comfort out of terror, righteousness out of sin, and life out of death." God made light to shine in darkness. God gives a Christian the power to do the same. We can turn afflictions into mercies. In the way that Jesus turned water into wine, we can turn the water of trouble into the wine of heavenly consolation.
—Jeremiah Burroughs
*Rare Jewel of Christian Contentment*

## JULY 23

## God's Grace

The only thing we need from God is mercy. God owes us nothing. We live upon free grace. Alexander gave a great gift to one of his subjects. The recipient was overwhelmed and protested, "I am not worthy of this." The king replied, "I do not give you this because you are worthy of it. I am giving a gift worthy of Alexander."

Whatever we have is not because we have earned it. It is freely given.

—Thomas Watson
*The Art of Divine Contentment*


## JULY 24

## Fretting is a Loss

Regardless of one's circumstances, a Christian may be as comfortable as though in heaven. Comfort is not the consequence of having much. Christ says, "One's life does not consist in the abundance of possessions" (Luke 12:15 NRSV). A bee is as satisfied with feeding from a flower as an ox grazing on the mountains. Happiness has nothing to do with well stocked barns. It has to do with a quiet mind and spirit.

Seneca assures us that a contented person is a happy person. Discontent is a fretting attitude that wastes and destroys the best we have. A drop or two of vinegar will turn a whole glass of wine sour. You

may have many blessings, but a drop or two of discontent will make all of them bitter. Discontent will keep you from enjoying what you already possess.
Why do you complain about your troubles? It is not trouble that troubles you, but discontentment. Water outside a ship does not sink it. It is the water that leaks inside that becomes a problem. Outward affliction need not sadden life. A contented spirit can sail above these waters. It takes a spiritual leak of discontent to endanger the soul.

—Thomas Watson
*The Art of Divine Contentment*

JULY 25

## Not Ordinary

We are not able to rest on this earth. There is no way a soul that is so weak and sinful, so intimately bound to such a neighbor as this flesh, could ever be satisfied. Soul-rest is freedom from sin, imperfection, and enemies. All of these continually pester us here. Christians often cry out in the language of Paul, "What a wretched man I am! Who will rescue me from this body of death?" (Romans 7:24).

Our flesh is not now those sun-like bodies which they shall be when this perishable clothes "itself with the imperishable, and the mortal with immortality" (1 Corinthians 15:53). Our bodies are our prisons and our burdens, full of infirmities and defects. We spend a lot of time repairing them and supplying what they need. Is it possible that an immortal soul should have rest in such a sick and noisy habitation?

The things we enjoy here are insufficient to satisfy our needs. Those who have the most of it have the greatest burden. Those who have a lot of it all ultimately cry out of its vanity and aggravation. We promise ourselves heaven upon earth; but when we come to enjoy it, it flies from us.

—Richard Baxter: *The Saints' Everlasting Rest*

JULY 26

## *My Symphony*

To live content with small means, to seek elegance rather than luxury, and refinement rather than fashion,
to be worthy, not respectable, and wealthy, not rich,
to study hard, think quietly, talk gently, act frankly,
to listen to stars and birds, to babes and sages, with open heart,
to bear all cheerfully, do all bravely, await occasions, hurry never,
in a word to let the spiritual, unbidden and unconscious, grow up through the common, this is to be my symphony.

—William Henry Channing: *My Symphony*

JULY 27
## *Steady*

Contentment is not something we get on our own. It is a fruit that does not grow in the garden of philosophy. It is a heavenly gift. "Godliness with contentment is great gain" (1 Timothy 6:6).

Contentment is habitual. It is a steady light in the soul. It does not appear intermittently like an infrequently seen star. It is a permanent condition. One action does not reveal true character. Even a stingy person might make a contribution. The generous person is one who regularly gives unselfishly. A contented person is one who is ordinarily content. It is not casual, but constant.

—Thomas Watson: *The Art of Divine Contentment*

JULY 28
## *Under Employed*

"Now Moses was tending the flock of Jethro his father-in-law, the priest of Midian" (Exodus 3:1). It may have annoyed Moses to be consigned to watching over a flock of sheep. He had great abilities. With such potential, he was busy with menial tasks. Some proud souls would crash. A truly great person goes ahead and stoops in humility. Moses kept the flocks of Jethro, and led them to the mountain of God. His humble submission resulted in much good.

—George Whitefield: *Memoirs*

JULY 29

## *Persisting*

"Let us run with perseverance the race marked out for us" (Hebrews 12:1). Even though the course is difficult and toilsome, we must hold out with patience and endure hardships. Though the journey is long, we must not stop short, but hold on until we arrive at the place we seek. Don't be discouraged with the length and problems of the trip. This is what happened to the freed Hebrew slaves on their way to the Promised Land. All of our thoughts and plans should be to press forward until we arrive. "Forgetting what is behind and straining toward what is ahead, I press on toward the goal to win the prize for which God has called me heavenward in Christ Jesus" (Philippians 3:13f).

Work at growing in divine love. Let this journey be an increasing flame in our hearts. Do the will of God on earth as the angels do it in heaven—in comfort and spiritual joy, in communion with God and Jesus Christ. "Like newborn babies, crave pure spiritual milk, so that by it you may grow up in your salvation" (1 Peter 2:2).
—Jonathan Edwards: *Works*


JULY 30

## *Frustrated Desires*

Sometimes God helps the spirit while postponing the desire of the flesh. Joseph spent years exiled in Egypt. He became a favorite prisoner of the jailer, and that must have given him some inward consolation, but he remained in jail. God alone knows what is expedient for us.

Sometimes he prolongs the deliverance of his chosen ones. Sometimes he even allows them to die at an early age. Who can doubt that John the Baptist wanted to see more of Christ's ministry, and to have been longer in conversation with him? Stephen would have been glad to work many more years preaching Christ's gospel, rather than suffer martyrdom as a young man. Whatever happens to our bodies, God will comfort our spirits and turn everything to our good—beyond our own expectation.

—John Knox: *A Treatise on Prayer*

JULY 31

## *Addition and Subtraction*

A Christian comes to contentment, not so much by way of addition, as by way of subtraction. The world has no skill in this, but we know that gratification comes not by adding to what we have, but rather by subtracting from our desires. This is the only way to equalize our desires and our circumstances.

Most people think they need to add to their possessions to gain contentment. If they have lost something, they look for something else to take up the slack. But happiness does not come this way. It is not the result of wanting more, but of wanting less.

—Jeremiah Burroughs
*Rare Jewel of Christian Contentment*

## AUGUST
*Prayer*

AUGUST 1

## God Listens to Prayer

The only people who realize the power of prayer are those who have experienced it. Praying when under duress is an important action. God always hears my most ardent prayers. I have received more than I sought. Sometimes there is a delay, but God never fails to answer.

A sincere prayer is a wonderful thing. It draws upon the power that is in God. An ordinary human can communicate with high and holy divinity. There is nothing to fear. God smiles upon us when we pray. There is no reason to let an awareness of our sinfulness interfere.

When you pray, understand that God is listening. Pray with faith in Christ. Prayer is an elevation of the heart to God.

—Martin Luther: *Table Talk*


AUGUST 2

## A Personal Prayer

God, I praise you for days well spent. I remain unsatisfied because I do not enjoy enough of you. I am too far from you. I want my soul more closely united to you by faith and love.

You know, Lord, that I want to love you above all things. You made me. You know my desires, my expectations. Every joy in me centers in you. It is you that I desire. It is your favor, your acceptance, your grace that I wish for more than anything else in the world. I rejoice in your glory. I rejoice in my relation to you. You are my Father, my Lord and my God. I thank you that you have brought me so far. I will be careful not to despair of your mercy at some time which is yet to come.

—Susanna Wesley: *Prayer*

AUGUST 3

## *Starting the Day*

Think of God at the beginning of a new day. This can be a natural thing. We could easily make a long list of subjects for prayer first thing in the morning.

The value of refreshing sleep
Our security while defenseless
Warm clothes waiting to be put on
The cheerful light of sunrise
The prospect of returning to friends
The possibility of serving God this new day
Welcoming an opportunity to learn something new

It is entirely proper at the lonely moment of waking to make natural expressions of joy and thankfulness to God. If we wake with such thoughts, even that is worthy of a prayer of praise. It could be the answer to a prayer we made when we went to bed the night before.

—Philip Doddridge
*The Rise and Progress of Religion*

AUGUST 4
## Preparation
"Those who seek the LORD lack no good thing" (Psalm 34:10). If what we want is good for us, we will have it. If it is not good, then not having it is good for us. Accepting the promise of Scripture brings pleasure.

Contentment prepares us for God's service. It oils the wheels of the soul and makes us fit for prayer and meditation. There is no way one who is overcome with the emotion of grief or discontent can "live in a right way in undivided devotion to the Lord" (1 Corinthians 7:35). Just as a violin is tuned before playing music, in the same way a Christian needs preparation for service and devotion. Discontent distracts our attention from God and focuses upon the present difficulty. Instead of your mind being on prayer, it is on your trouble.

—Thomas Watson
*The Art of Divine Contentment*

AUGUST 5
## Remember to Pray
Do not forget to go to God in prayer. If left to yourself, your own wisdom and strength, you will be insufficient for your own security. You will always be in danger from your own imagination and the other enemies of your soul. Commit the keeping of your soul to God every day. Be particularly careful

to remember to pray when a special hazard threatens you. Humbly seek God to be your help.

—Charles Chauncy
*Enthusiasm Described and Cautioned Against*

AUGUST 6

## The Necessity of Prayer

It has been suggested that prayer is unnecessary if God already knows everything. This misses the point. The purpose of prayer is not to tell God something he doesn't know. Prayer allows us to communicate with God. Our active participation is important. "Ask and it will be given to you; seek and you will find; knock and the door will be opened to you" (Matthew 7:7).

—Hannah More: *Practical Piety*

AUGUST 7

## First Prayer of the Day

Let God have your first waking thoughts. Reverently and thankfully lift up your heart to him for the rest you enjoyed. Cast yourself upon him for the day ahead. Become so familiar with this practice that your conscience may check you when common thoughts intrude. Think of the mercy of a night's rest. Many others in the world had a difficult night. They were in cold, hard lodgings and suffering from agonizing pain and sickness, weary of their beds and of their lives.

Some did not wake this morning. Think how quickly days and nights are rolling on. Observe that which is lacking in the preparedness of your soul and seek to improve it without delay.

—Richard Baxter: *Works*

AUGUST 8

## *Giving Thanks*

We should never cease praising and thanking God because God never stops giving to us. We do not have to look far to find a reason for gratitude. When we recognize that God provides us with every good that comes our way, we give him the honor that is due. It is not right for us to enjoy God's benefits without being grateful. When David experienced the Lord's love he said, "He put a new song in my mouth, a hymn of praise to our God" (Psalm 40:3). This implies that silence is an unacceptable response. Let no blessing pass without praise. Every blessing God gives is a new reason for thanksgiving.

When we are tired, impatient, afraid, grieving, or despondent, our prayers may be little more than morose murmuring. Paul instructs us to thank God even before we receive what we want. "In everything, by prayer and petition, with thanksgiving, present your requests to God" (Philippians 4:6).

—John Calvin: *Of Prayer*

AUGUST 9

## *The Material of Prayer*

Let us boldly ask God for whatever is necessary. Ask for health and sustenance, for defense from misery, for deliverance from trouble, for peace among nations, for success in our vocation. Ask God for everything.

By seeking and receiving such things we have a taste of God's sweetness, and become inflamed with his love.

—John Knox: *A Treatise on Prayer*

AUGUST 10

## *Best Prayer*

Sometimes a Christian thinks, "I can't pray as eloquently as others." Grace is beyond gifts. You are comparing your grace with someone else's gifts. There is a vast difference between them. Grace without gifts is far more desirable than gifts without grace. Perhaps you can't speak of religious ideas as fluently as some other person you know. Religious experience is beyond argument and words. Judas may have been able to tell others all about Jesus, but the woman in Luke 8:47, who experienced his power, is way ahead. A sanctified heart is better than a silver tongue. Gifts and grace are as different as a tulip painted on a wall and one flowering in the garden.

You say you cannot pray as elegantly as others. Prayer lives better in the heart than in the head. It is more important that a prayer be fervent than fluent.

God is more attracted to a lively spirit than to beauty of speech. The one praying is not delivering a speech. Sighs and groans are the best rhetoric for prayer.
—Thomas Watson: *The Art of Divine Contentment*

AUGUST 11

## Prayer is a Privilege

Faith leads us to understand that God is our Father. We respond to his love; we learn that he is always ready to hear from us. It is easy to pray when we know God cares and is eager to help.

There is no bold impudence in a Christian's approach to God. Don't imagine you are doing anything rash when you pray. You are invited. Your worthiness has nothing to do with it.

Prayer is an indication of faith. Failure to pray is a sign of a lack of faith. When we understand God is waiting for the prayers we have a privilege to offer, we will not hesitate. We will regularly call for God's assistance. We are his adopted children.
—John Calvin: *The Privilege of Prayer*

AUGUST 12

## Vital Prayer

"Come near to God and he will come near to you" (James 4:8). A life of steady prayer will obtain every spiritual blessing. Avoid formality when you pray. Many think anything said to God must be carefully expressed in well-chosen words. This is not what I consider prayer. When you pray, use the same honesty and earnestness you would use in asking a friend for something you really want.

Expect an answer. Many pray without even thinking about an answer. How can they expect to receive one? You would not grant a favor to anyone without waiting a moment for a reply. If you are serious about your spiritual life, turn to God every day (I almost said every hour). Think carefully about how some of your prayers may have been answered in ways you did not expect.

Be thankful to God. Pray earnestly. Believe that what you ask of him in the name of Christ, you shall eventually receive. This will invigorate your prayers.

—Hannah Sinclair: *A Letter to Catherine*

AUGUST 13

## *Prayer in Adversity*

The hurts of life can actually work for good. They get our attention and teach important lessons. God makes our adversity our university.

Afflictions teach us to pray better. Jonah was asleep in the ship, but awake and in prayer in the whale's belly. When God tests us with fire, our hearts boil over. Nothing is more pleasing to God than to have his children praying fervently. David, that sweet singer of Israel, tuned his harp most melodiously and prayed his strongest prayers when he was in great difficulty.

—Thomas Watson: *The Art of Divine Contentment*

AUGUST 14

## *Patience in Prayer*

God will hear every prayer that springs from faith in Christ. But God does not permit us to dictate the amount, the way, or the time for his answer. Our ideas can place no limitations on divine activity.

St. Augustine's mother asked God to convert her son. When there were no immediate results, she began to ask others to pressure him into the faith. She was frantic about this for years and could see no results. When God understood the right time had come, he transformed Augustine into one of the great lights of the church.

"The prayer of the righteous is powerful and effective" (James 5:16 NRSV). Prayer is influential because God is committed to it.

—Martin Luther: *Table Talk*

AUGUST 15

## *Prayer Purges*

Prayer is a safety valve. It releases dangerous pressure, like opening a vein to let out bad blood. When we are unhappy and disturbed, prayer brings relief. It is like a key that unlocks our soul and allows whatever disturbs us to flow away. Prayer unloads the spirit and turns our problems over to God.

When we share our concerns with a friend there is a similar easing and quieting of our emotions. Our relief comes by sharing rather than by strong resolutions. Prayer brings the strength of Christ into the soul. Paul tells us he could be content in every condition, but he was not able to do that by himself. He said, "I can do everything through him who gives me strength" (Philippians 4:13).

—Thomas Watson
*The Art of Divine Contentment*

AUGUST 16

# Psalm 86

> Lord bend to me your ear
>   And me hear
> Most poor, and most oppressed
> O save my soul distressed
> Who deeply is your debtor
> Save me and make my bad state better
>   For you my God I serve.
> From you my hope does never swerve.
>
> Lord pity on me take
>   For I make

To you my daily crying
My heart in sorrow lying
With joy O Lord re-comfort
For unto you my only comfort
My soul does strive to rise
With stretched hands and bended eyes.
—Mary Sidney: *The Sidney Psalter*

AUGUST 17

## *Defensive Prayer*

People respond to adversity in different ways. They think they can help themselves by swearing and abusing others. Someone annoys them and they have no way to defend themselves except through anger and bitter words. They attempt to relieve stress in this manner.

When devout persons are in a difficult situation, relief comes another way. Their stress, frustration, and pain are as great as that of anyone else. Instead of outrage and cursing, they turn to God in prayer. They open their hearts to God, letting out sorrows and fears. They come away from prayer with a joyful expression on their faces. Scripture says of Hannah that "she went her way and ate something, and her face was no longer downcast" (I Samuel 1:18).

—Jeremiah Burroughs
*Rare Jewel of Christian Contentment*

## AUGUST 18

## *A Leader Prays*

I often found Martin Luther weeping and praying for the whole church. He spent a part of almost every day reading the Psalms, with which he mingled his own supplications accompanied by tears and groans. He often expressed indignation at those who were too busy to pray. He explained this is why God produced different forms of prayer. When we read a prayer our minds respond with prayers of their own. God was his anchor, and faith never failed him.

—Philip Melanchthon
*Oration at Funeral of Martin Luther*

## AUGUST 19

## *Prayer for Love*

Lord, give us hearts that will never forget your love. Let us always live in your love, whether we sleep or wake, live or die. Your love is eternal life and everlasting rest. Let its flame always burn in us. Let it grow and brighten until our souls are glowing and shining with warm light. Be our joy, our hope, our strength, our shield and shepherd.

Our happiness consists in continuing in your love. Your name and essence are love. Burn in our hearts. Enlighten our understanding. Sanctify our wills. Fill all of our thoughts.

—Johann Arndt
*Sechs Bücher vom Wahren Christenthum*

AUGUST 20

## The Elements of Prayer

Prayer is communication with God. We can share our desires, our joys, our sighs, and every thought we have with God. When you pray, try to descend in the depth of your heart, seeking God.

True prayer is pure affection. Dismiss all thought of your own glory, dignity, and self-confidence. Come to God like a child to a parent. "Ask and it will be given to you; seek and you will find; knock and the door will be opened to you" (Matthew 7:7).

—John Calvin: *Instruction in Faith*

AUGUST 21

## Neglecting Prayer

The person who neglects prayer understands nothing of faith. If fire is without heat or a burning lamp is without light, then true faith may be without fervent prayer. Anyone who has no desire to seek God's support and help is little different from someone who makes false gods. The person who does not pray in a time of trouble denies God; he is like a sick person who has no doctor, or who refuses to take medication. Failure to pray is an admission that you do not know God.

—John Knox: *A Treatise on Prayer*

AUGUST 22

## *Prayer Defined*

>Prayer is need seeking relief.
>Prayer is sin speaking to the only one who can grant pardon.
>Prayer is earnestness rather than eloquence.
>Prayer is faith speaking to mercy.
>Prayer is the soul drawing close to God.
>Prayer is both rational and emotional.
>—Hannah More: *Practical Piety*

AUGUST 23

## *Fill Your Day with Prayer*

It is not possible for us to think always of God. "Pray continually" (1 Thessalonians 5:17) is a noble goal, but our human weakness makes it an unlikely achievement. The next best thing is to set specific times during the day for prayer. During these designated moments concentrate entirely upon your prayer. Let nothing distract you.

Good times to set for yourself include when you wake in the morning, when you begin your day's work, when you sit down to eat, and when you go to bed. The most important thing to remember is that such a practice is not a task we do to please God. Observing such times of prayer, moreover, does not free you from the necessity of prayer at other moments of the day. The practice is nothing other than a concession to human weakness.

—John Calvin: *Of Prayer*

AUGUST 24

## Honest Prayer

Honestly desire what you ask of God. Nothing is more odious before God than hypocrisy and pretending. It is wrong to ask God for something you don't need, or for something you think you will obtain from another source. How silly to ask God to forgive you when you expect you will be able to earn that forgiveness by your good works! Such a prayer mocks God. You are deceiving yourself. Ask for nothing you do not know is beyond your reach. Depend upon the mercy of God.

—John Knox: *A Treatise on Prayer*


AUGUST 25

## A Way to Begin

The practice of private morning devotion varies from person to person. You will need to find your own way. If I could design a model for someone with half an hour or more to give to this practice, it would be something like this:Start with praise and thanksgiving for God's mercies in Christ. Do this with genuine sincerity. Praising God without enthusiasm is not to praise him at all. Renew your dedication to God. Promise to live this day to God's glory. Consider what the day may have in store for you. Will there be any opportunities for doing or receiving good? Will there be any temptations likely?

After this review, offer a brief prayer seeking God's assistance.

Then read a few verses of Scripture. Select something from the most helpful parts. Read them devotionally and not as a student. Pray over what you are reading. A good way to finish your devotions would be with a psalm, a hymn, or a sacred poem.

—Philip Doddridge
*The Rise and Progress of Religion*

AUGUST 26

## *Private Prayer*

Jesus said, "When you pray, go into your room, close the door and pray to your Father, who is unseen" (Matthew 6:6). Private prayer really does not require a special place. Christ was instructing us not to make a vain public show of our prayers. Being seen by others can distract us from actual prayer.

Our Lord himself observed no special place for prayer. Sometimes he prayed on the Mount of Olives, sometimes in the desert, sometimes in the temple, and sometimes in a garden. Peter prayed on a housetop. Paul prayed in prison. We can pray anywhere, any time.

—John Knox: *A Treatise on Prayer*

AUGUST 27

## Genuine Prayer

Trouble and difficulty produce the best prayers. "Call upon me in the day of trouble" (Psalm 50:15). Serious problems put an end to religious chatter. Honest prayer begins to emerge from the heart. Hard times teach us to pray.

Gatherings of Christians may sometimes recite formal prayers like croaking frogs. We can say prayers without devotion, without even understanding the words we speak. It exercises the tongue, but the soul is not involved.

There is no need for us to speak all of our prayers aloud. We can pray silently without interruption. Even a sigh can be a prayer. "The groaning of the needy" (Psalm 12:5) captured God's attention and resulted in divine action.

—Martin Luther: *Table Talk*

AUGUST 28

## Prayer from the Pit

Prayer is an earnest conversation with God. We tell God how things are with us, asking for his help, and thank him for every good we have received. The Psalms of David are examples of prayers that include these things.

Trouble and fear are excellent nudges to prayer. When we have no idea that another person can help us, and we know that we are beyond helping ourselves, we naturally call to God for comfort and support. Prayer from a deep pit of tribulation ascends into God's presence, and it is not lost.

—John Knox: *A Treatise on Prayer*

AUGUST 29

## *Short Prayers*

Much prayer is contained in this single sentence: "Give us today our daily bread" (Matthew 6:11). Pray as you feel the need. Praying a brief prayer like this, with faith, is better than reciting the entire Psalter without faith.

Each word of this sentence is significant. But the word "bread" represents everything necessary to sustain life. All of the essentials are contained in this one little word.

—Hugh Latimer: *Fruitful Sermons*

AUGUST 30

## *Christ's Teaching on Prayer*

With a few excellent words, the Lord's Prayer demonstrates the full spectrum of prayer. It begins with great respect for the mystery of heavenly things no earthly mind will ever fully comprehend. It moves on to everyday needs, And it deals with the evil within us. Wisdom itself produced such a prayer. Only God could have given it to us.

The Lord's Prayer unites us. It leads us to pray for each other. It permits us to pray together. Prayer preserves the church.

Christ says, "Ask and it will be given to you; seek and you will find; knock and the door will be opened to you" (Matthew 7:7). He also teaches us that we are to be persistent in prayer. Sometimes we must keep on knocking and knocking before God responds.

—Martin Luther: *Table Talk*


AUGUST 31

## *The Attitude of Prayer*

True repentance comes before prayer. There can be no sincere calling on God's name without it. "When you spread out your hands in prayer, I will hide my eyes from you; even if you offer many prayers, I will not listen. Your hands are full of blood; wash and make yourselves clean. Take your evil deeds out of my sight! Stop doing wrong" (Isaiah 1:15—16).

Don't imagine that some goodness in ourselves qualifies our prayers as worth hearing. Boasting of your high morality actually repels God's mercy. Read about the Pharisee in Luke 18. The most holy prayers are humble prayers. There is no mention of the merits of the one praying. The only thing such prayers depend upon is the mercy of God.

—John Knox: *A Treatise on Prayer*

## SEPTEMBER
*Inner Life*

SEPTEMBER 1

## It Takes Time

Spiritual development is a gradual work. The change from sin to holiness, from love of the world to love of God, does not happen in an instant. It resembles the light of morning that grows brighter and brighter with the passage of time. "The path of the righteous is like the first gleam of dawn, shining ever brighter till the full light of day" (Proverbs 4:18).

—Hannah Sinclair: *A Letter to Catherine*

SEPTEMBER 2

## The Mystery of Godliness

"Beyond all question, the mystery of godliness is great: He appeared in a body, was vindicated by the Spirit, was seen by angels, was preached among the nations, was believed on in the world, was taken up in glory" (1 Timothy 3:16). This is a hidden thing. Incredibly, God appeared in a body and became one of us. This surpasses our ability to understand. It is astonishing.

Not only did the majesty of God come near us, he became one of us. God joined us in the person of our Lord Jesus Christ. Christ is both God and human. He has bridged a vast chasm. Human flesh offers little but wretchedness and misery; it is a bottomless pit of stench and infection. And yet, in Jesus Christ, we see the glory of God, who is worshiped by angels, as well as human weakness.

This is a secret and hidden thing. The angels themselves could not have thought it up.
—John Calvin: *The Mystery of Godliness*

SEPTEMBER 3

## *An Experience of Faith*

I worried that I would fall from grace and lose my soul. The Spirit strongly impressed on my mind to enter into my closet and carry my case once more to the Lord. The Lord enabled me to draw close to him in an extraordinary manner. While I wrestled with him for the victory over this self-doubt, there appeared a form of fire, about the size of a man's hand, as I was on my knees. At the same moment, there appeared to the eye of faith a man robed in white from shoulders to feet. He said, "You shall never turn from the cross."

Since that time I have never doubted. I believe that God will keep me until the day of redemption. Nothing "will be able to separate us from the love of God that is in Christ Jesus our Lord" (Romans 8:39).
—Jarena Lee: *Life and Religious Experience*

SEPTEMBER 4

## *With God at Work*

Here are directions for maintaining your devotional life. Scripture describes it as being "filled with delight day after day, rejoicing always in his presence"

(Proverbs 8:30). We need to remember God even as we take care of the day's necessary secular business. With an awareness of God our work will be better. We will not labor sluggishly or haphazardly. We will not take three hours to do the work of one hour. We will try to accomplish as much as we can with each hour, using precious time as the limited gift it is. Always remember that we need God's blessing to make our work successful.

—Philip Doddridge
*The Rise and Progress of Religion*

SEPTEMBER 5

## Kingdom Within

A Christian carries tremendous resources. People will not say, "'Here it is,' or 'There it is,' because the kingdom of God is within you" (Luke 17:21). When a king travels, he does not worry about his circumstances in a foreign place. He realizes he has a kingdom of his own. Because the kingdom of God is within you, God is in your soul. The soul enjoys communion with Christ.

This is difficult to express. Only those who experience it understand the meaning. The point is that here and now, in this life, you have the capacity for a powerful manifestation of the spiritual presence of God. You do not have to wait for heaven to become familiar with that kingdom. The only soul that will ever go to heaven will be the soul to which heaven has already come.

—Jeremiah Burroughs
*Rare Jewel of Christian Contentment*

SEPTEMBER 6

## *Fear Not*

There are a variety of ways to express religious faith. Most of us are not really in awe of God, and yet many of us have an idea that there is a divinity of some kind who has great power. Some believe because they are afraid not to believe. Still, they live in a disorderly and dishonest manner. They have no regard for the judgment of God. Their cautious anxiety actually turns them away from God. They may even attempt to serve God with great care, but they do not worship the eternal God. God is nothing more to them than the dreams and fancies of their own imaginations.

True piety does not consist in a fear that wants to run away from God. True piety is a pure and genuine love for God. With this, it is not necessary to think of escaping God.

—John Calvin: *Instruction in Faith*

SEPTEMBER 7

## *Perfect Love*

Perfect love is a kind of self-neglect. It is a wandering out of ourselves, a voluntary death. The lover dies to himself and his personal interests. He doesn't think about them or care for them anymore. The important thing is pleasing and gratifying the object of love. A person who is thoroughly in love is quite upset if love is not returned. When love is returned, he can begin to pay attention to his own business, not because the business is his, but because the beloved is pleased to share an interest in it. The one who is loved becomes dear to himself because he is dear to another.

—Henry Scougal
*The Life of God in the Soul of Man*


SEPTEMBER 8

## *Resentment*

Dislike what deserves it, but never hate. Hate is almost always directed at persons rather than things. Malice is one of the blackest sins in the soul.

We must try to bind and qualify our resentments with love to the offender. Then our anger would be without sin, and actually help the guilty. Love alone could make it lawful.

Not to be provoked is best, but if you can't help it, at least wait until the fuming is over before you offer a correction. Every stroke our fury strikes will certainly strike back at us.

Passion is a fever of the mind, which leaves us weaker than it found us.

—William Penn: *Some Fruits of Solitude*

SEPTEMBER 9

## *Examine Yourself*

Here is how to do a spiritual self-examination. Empty your mind of all other cares and thoughts. Let there be no mental distractions. This work will take all of your attention.

Choose a proper time and place. Let the place be private, and the time when interruptions are least likely to disturb you. If possible, let it be the present time.

Have some Scripture handy—either in memory or in writing. Fall down before God in vigorous prayer. Desire the assistance of God's Spirit. Ask to discover the truth about your spiritual condition. Ask if you are sincere. If you hesitate, force your prayers on. Don't trifle away the time. Do as the Psalmist: "My heart mused and my spirit inquired" (Psalm 77:6). If you can prevail with yourself, you will also prevail with God.

—Richard Baxter: *The Saints' Everlasting Rest*

SEPTEMBER 10

## *Experiencing the Spirit*

The blind have a much more acute sense of hearing than those who can see. Their sense of feeling is exceedingly fine. People like me develop similar skills. I have never had more than three months of schooling. Because I wanted to know much about God, I have watched the operations of the Spirit very closely. As a result, the Spirit has led me. But let me state that the Spirit has never led me contrary to the Scriptures. "All who are led by the Spirit of God are children of God" (Romans 8:14 NRSV).

—Jarena Lee: *Life and Religious Experience*

SEPTEMBER 11

## *Perfect Union*

God has made us for himself. Of him, and through him, and to him are all things. Therefore, union with God is our highest achievement. In this world that union will always remain imperfect. Much darkness limits our knowledge of God. An abundance of estrangement mingles with our conformity to God. Here we can serve and glorify God, but in a very imperfect manner. Sin which dishonors God mingles with our service.

Perfect union with God will be experienced in heaven. Then we will have clear views of God. There we shall be fully conformed to God, without any remaining sin. We will see him as he is. We will serve God perfectly and glorify him in an exalted manner. Then we shall perfectly give ourselves to God. Our hearts will be pure and holy offerings, presented in a flame of divine love.

—Jonathan Edwards: *Works*

SEPTEMBER 12

## *The Heart*

The Bible often speaks of the heart as a fountain, the source of moral decisions and the activity of the soul. "For out of the heart come evil thoughts, murder, adultery, sexual immorality, theft, false testimony, slander" (Matthew 15:19). This is a figurative use of the term, which recognizes an analogy between the heart of the body and the heart of the soul

The fleshly organ of the body, by its constant action, pumps life through one's system. The spiritual heart is the fountain of spiritual life. It is a deep-seated but voluntary preference of the mind, and it is behind all of our voluntary activity and emotions. We have control over it. A change of heart consists in changing the controlling preference of the mind—a change from selfishness to benevolence, from having supreme regard for your own interest to a controlling choice of the glory of God and his kingdom.

—Charles Finney: *Sermons on Important Subjects*

SEPTEMBER 13

## *Reach Higher*

It is enough for us to have a little knowledge of divine things. We should be content with what light we are given. Our own judgment is weak. We look forward to the day when we will see more clearly. "Now we see but a poor reflection; then we shall see face to face. Now I know in part; then I shall know fully" (1 Corinthians 13:12).

When you deal with spiritual mysteries, remember not to flatter yourself by thinking you have sufficient knowledge and ability to understand a matter so vast. Learn to climb up beyond yourself. Revere that majesty that passes our understanding. Strive to profit from every little grain of divine knowledge you do receive.

—John Calvin: *The Mystery of Godliness*

SEPTEMBER 14

## Comfortable with Yourself

The one whose soul is filled with good spiritual things is like someone with a comfortable home and happy family. Such a person enjoys being at home. God grants pleasant surroundings and companions. Those who have quarreling and distress at home often think of going out with friends to escape an unhappy situation. A spouse moans, complains, and finds fault. Any excuse to go out is welcomed because there is no peace at home.

Worldly people have the same restlessness of spirit. Augustine compares a bad conscience with a scolding wife. Such a person does not care to look into his own soul. He would rather be out, looking at other things. When there is nothing beautiful within yourself you will prefer to be distracted as much as possible.

—Jeremiah Burroughs
*Rare Jewel of Christian Contentment*

SEPTEMBER 15

## *Inner Struggle*

While we live here, we struggle with inner conflict. What Paul calls "the flesh" strives against "the spirit." We attempt to bring the natural and corrupt affections we have in us into obedience to the spirit. At the very least, we bridle them in order to keep them from ruling and having dominion over us.

Only the devout experience this inner strife. If you feel it, rejoice. It indicates your name is "written in the Lamb's book of life" (Revelation 21:27).

—John Bradford: *The Flesh and the Spirit*

SEPTEMBER 16

## *Taking Stock*

None of us are so wicked that we are beyond help. Look inside yourself. What are your secrets? How have you spent your days? If you find some ugliness in yourself, ask God to forgive you. Your prayer will certainly be answered. God will be true to his promise and forgive your sins. He sent his only Son into the world to save sinners like you.

Think of God's great love. Amend your life. Avoid temptation. If you will do this, none of the sins you have committed will harm or condemn you. The mercy of God is greater than all the sins in the world.

—Hugh Latimer: *Fruitful Sermons*

SEPTEMBER 17

## *Perfection is Possible*

The commandment to "love the Lord your God with all your heart and with all your soul and with all your mind" (Matthew 22:37) is possible. You really can "love your neighbor as yourself" (Matthew 22:39). The Word of God would not ask us to do something that is beyond our ability. This is the life God intends us to have and it can be done. The seed of it is a hidden treasure in each human soul.

The mystery of a secret inward life is our most precious possession. Religion must never be an outward observance. The power and operation of an inward life of God in our souls is not fanaticism or mere enthusiasm. Scripture teaches that the kingdom of heaven is within us.

—William Law: *Mystical Writings*

SEPTEMBER 18

## Absorbed in God

When you perceive you are knit to God, and your soul is more tightly bonded to him than to your own body, then you will know his everlasting, and inconceivable, and indescribable goodness. You will see the true nobleness of your soul that came from God and was made to be reunited to him.

Entering into Jesus, you plunge into an infinite sea of goodness. This goodness more easily drowns and happily swallows you than the ocean does a drop of water. Then you are hid and transformed in him. You shall be thinking without thought, and knowing without knowledge, and loving without love, completely understood by one you cannot comprehend.

—Robert Leighton
*Rules and Instructions for a Holy Life*


SEPTEMBER 19

## Almost Persuaded

"Almost thou persuadest me to be a Christian" (Acts 26:28 KJV). There are many who go this far. There is heathen honesty in the statement. They follow good rules of conduct. They do not steal their neighbor's goods. They do not oppress the poor. They do not extort, cheat, or defraud others. They regard truth as well as justice.

Those who are almost Christian may have the form of godliness, the outside of a real Christian. The almost Christian does nothing the Bible forbids. He attends church. He takes communion seriously. He prays at home.

Only sincerity is missing. By sincerity I mean a real, inward principle of religion that produces these outward actions.

—John Wesley: *The Almost Christian*

SEPTEMBER 20

## *Spontaneous Devotion*

True religion is a union of the soul with God. It is a genuine participation of the Divine nature, the very image of God drawn upon the soul. "I no longer live, but Christ lives in me" (Galatians 2:20). Religion is a divine life. It is an inward, free, and self-moving principle. External motives and threats do not control anyone who experiences this union. It is not a matter of being bribed by promises or constrained by laws. It is a powerful inclination to live well and to enjoy it.

Loving and serving God becomes a natural inclination. Prayer, thanksgiving, and repentance do not result from a command, but from an awareness of personal need and divine goodness. Charity is not forced. Love makes giving likely.

—Henry Scougal: *The Life of God in the Soul of Man*

SEPTEMBER 21

## *High Principles Require Life*

Beware of betraying the innocent among you with what appears to be the truth. If it is the truth without the life, you betray your own souls. Turn to the pure eternal principle of the Lord God. Pay attention to God that you may see your Savior and that your souls may live. You receive God's free grace. Let it be your teacher and leader.

—Margaret Fell Fox
*Epistle to Convinced Friends, 1656*


SEPTEMBER 22

## *A Square Circle*

Loveless teachers are not able to have the spiritual gifts Paul mentions: speaking with tongues, prophesying, understanding mysteries, moving mountains with faith, giving their possessions to the poor, and allowing themselves to be burned. When love is absent, such individuals are proud, resentful, puffed up, impatient, unstable, dishonest, cruel, skeptical, mean, scornful, bitter, reluctant to serve, suspicious, selfish, ruthless, and arrogant.

There is no way such people are going to move mountains with their faith. They certainly will never consider sacrificing themselves for Christ. Paul presents an impossible proposition in the thirteenth chapter of First Corinthians. He is telling us that since they do not have love, neither do they really possess those gifts. They merely assume the name and appearance.

—Martin Luther: *Sermon on Christian Love*

SEPTEMBER 23

## *God Gives Understanding*

After we have said everything we can say, the secret mysteries of a new nature and divine life will not be sufficiently expressed. Language lacks the capacity to reach these mysteries. They will never be understood by anyone who is not burning within and awake to the sense of spiritual things. "Truly it is the spirit in a mortal, the breath of the Almighty, that makes for understanding" (Job 32:8 NRSV).

—Henry Scougal
*The Life of God in the Soul of Man*

SEPTEMBER 24

## *Increasing Devotion*

I went to Mayfair Chapel and heard prayers and an excellent sermon from the Book of Job on the comforts of piety. I was in a fine frame. I thought that God really designed us to be happy. I shall certainly be a religious old man. I was much so in youth. I have now and then flashes of devotion, and it will one day burn with a steady flame.

—James Boswell: *London Journal*

SEPTEMBER 25

## *Beginning the Day*

As you begin your day, consider your insensitivity to God. Keep in mind that God is always seeking you, eager for your response. Say to your soul, "Wake up and move!" Follow God. Live this day in a way that pleases God. Think of this day's work as an assignment from God. Ask God to help you make the best of today's opportunities. Do everything for the glory of God and the welfare of others.

—John Bradford: *Daily Meditations*

SEPTEMBER 26

## *Discovering Truth*

I did not learn Christianity all at once. I was tempted to look deeper and deeper for a true understanding of Holy Scripture. St. Paul was tormented with a need to study Holy Scripture. Hanging on my neck were the pope, the universities, the scholars, and the devil. These forced me into the Bible. I read with careful perseverance. After a long time, God be praised, I attained a true understanding of it. Without that kind of driving force we are only religious speculators. We reason and dream the best we can. But the Holy Scripture is certain and true. May God give me the ability to catch hold of its proper use.

—Martin Luther: *Table Talk*

SEPTEMBER 27

## Restricted Range

There are Christians who are obsessed with defending what they call orthodoxy. They attend worship services regularly and behave fairly decently. They avoid overindulgence in anything. They are careful not to do too much for Christ. They do not want to appear to be fanatics. They dread enthusiasm more than anything else. They maintain their religious life by repeating certain religious acts. They are content to remain as they are. They have reached their goal. They hold their ground without bothering to look for some imaginary perfection.

—Hannah More: *Practical Piety*


SEPTEMBER 28

## Religious Pretense

There are so many pretenders to religion that few understand what it really means. Some place it in the intellect, in orthodox notions and opinions. The only account they can give of their religion is that they belong to this or that denomination or have joined one of the many sects that have divided believers.

Still others put all religion in the emotions, in rapture and ecstatic devotion. Their goal is to pray with passion, to think of heaven with pleasure, and to court their Savior. They consider themselves to be in love with Jesus and assume a great confidence of their salvation, which they prize most highly.

These practices of piety are mistaken for the whole of religion.

—Henry Scougal
*The Life of God in the Soul of Man*

SEPTEMBER 29

## *Opinions*

I will not quarrel with you about any opinion. Only see that your heart is right toward God, that you know and love the Lord Jesus Christ, that you love your neighbor and walk as your Master walked. I desire nothing more.

I am sick of opinions. I am weary of them. My soul loathes this frothy food. Give me solid and substantial religion. Give me someone who is a humble, gentle lover of God. I want to associate with individuals who are full of mercy and good fruits, who are not hypocrites, who have the patience of hope. Let my soul be with these Christians wherever they are, and whatever opinion they may have. God asks, "Who is this that darkens my counsel with words without knowledge?" (Job 38:2).

—John Wesley: *Works*

SEPTEMBER 30

# The Power of the Name

The only thing I know about Jesus is his name. I have not seen or heard him. Yet I have, God be praised, learned so much about him from the Scriptures that I am completely satisfied. I have no desire to see or hear him in the body. It was when I was forsaken and deserted by everyone, in my greatest weakness, in fear and trembling, when persecuted by the wicked world, that I experienced most deeply the divine power which this name, Christ Jesus, communicated to me.

—Martin Luther: *Table Talk*

# OCTOBER
*Scripture*

OCTOBER 1

## Use of the Bible

Study the Bible diligently. It is not enough to read through it. Give its pages careful study. Try to determine a passage's meaning. Compare one verse with another. Ask God to inspire your study.

Meditate often upon Christ. Consider not only what he has done for you, but also what you can do for him. Try to ask as sincerely as David, "How can I repay the LORD for all his goodness to me?" (Psalm 116:12). Let your look to Jesus be a look of gratitude and imitation. Read with the utmost care his life, his teaching, and the writings of the apostles. This will guide you to determine the best ways to show your gratitude. You will learn to live to him who died for you.

—Hannah Sinclair: *A Letter to Catherine*


OCTOBER 2

## Scripture as a Standard

Keep close to the Scripture. Attribute nothing to the Holy Spirit that does not agree with it. Compare the motions of your mind and the workings of your excitable imagination with the rule of God's Word. Be impartial about this. Don't bend the Bible to make it fit your preconceived ideas. Turn to the Bible with a willingness to know the truth as it lies plainly in the Scripture itself.

Have reverence for this book of God. Make it the great rule of judgment. You can avoid being deluded by doing this. What does the Bible say? If your imagined spiritual motions do not agree with Scripture, you have not been guided by the Spirit. They are only the workings of your mind, or something worse.

—Charles Chauncy
*Enthusiasm Described and Cautioned Against*

OCTOBER 3

# Psalm 119

> O what a lantern, what a lamp of light
>     Is your pure Word to me
> To clear my paths and guide my goings right
>     I swear and swear again
> I of your statutes will observer be
>     You justly do ordain.
>
> The heavy weights of grief oppress me sore
>     Lord, raise me by your Word
> As you to me did promise heretofore
>     And this unforced praise
> I for an offering bring, Accept O Lord
>     And show to me your ways.

—Mary Sidney: *The Sidney Psalter*

OCTOBER 4
## Bible Versions
Various translations of the Scriptures do not result in divisions among the faithful. It is healthy for the people of God to have many different translations of the Bible. From the earliest centuries there have been divergent renderings of the sacred text. When people are not able to read it in the original languages, it is important that they can have it in their own tongue. They should work diligently, translating out of one language into another. Instead of being offended by their work, we should thank God for their devotion.
—Miles Coverdale: *A Prologue to the Bible*

OCTOBER 5
## A Welcomed Bible
God showed mercy on me in my captivity by sending me a Bible. One of the Indians returned from a fight with some plunder. He asked me if I would like to have the Bible that was in his basket. I asked if they would let me read it and he answered affirmatively. I accepted the Bible.

In that sad time it occurred to me to begin by reading Deuteronomy 28. As I read I understood that there would be no mercy for me. The blessings were gone. Curses had replaced them. I had missed my opportunity. But the Lord helped me to continue reading until I came to chapter 30. There was a promise of mercy.

If we would return to him by repentance, though we be scattered far and wide, the Lord would bring us together again. I will never forget this Scripture as long as I live. It comforted me greatly.

—Mary Rowlandson
*Narrative of Captivity and Restoration*

OCTOBER 6

## Scripture Fragments

The Word of God deserves such reverence that we ought not to hesitate to submit ourselves to it. There are always those who question the authority of the Bible. They may admit that it is so majestic that we ought to bow before it, but they still speak against portions of it.

We are not at liberty to pick and choose which passages of the Bible we will accept. This is only partially obeying God. The whole Scripture is important. "All Scripture is God-breathed and is useful for teaching, rebuking, correcting and training in righteousness" (2 Timothy 3:16). We are to receive the whole Bible without exception.

—John Calvin: *The Proper Use of Scripture*

OCTOBER 7

## Faith on Trial

As I deeply pondered my difficulties with the church, I thought of a text of Scripture that tells us whoever denies that Jesus Christ has come in the flesh "is the antichrist—he denies the Father and the Son" (1 John 2:22). I could not easily understand what this meant. Only the Lord could open the Scripture for me. God revealed the truth to me by the voice of his own Spirit to my soul.

The Lord then led me to a reassuring Scripture. "Do not fear, O Jacob my servant; do not be dismayed, O Israel. I will surely save you out of a distant place, your descendants from the land of their exile" (Jeremiah 46:27). You have power over my body, but the Lord Jesus has power over both my body and my soul. Having seen God, I am not afraid of what you can do to me. God delivered Daniel out of the lion's den. He will deliver me.

—Anne Hutchinson: *Trial Transcript*

OCTOBER 8

## *Purpose*

The purpose of the Word of God is not to teach us how to talk, to make us eloquent and subtle, but to reform our lives. If you want to know if the gospel has made any difference in someone's life, notice whether or not that person's behavior corresponds with the written Word of God.

St. Paul encourages us to let the Bible be our guide. We can model our lives by it "so that everyone who

belongs to God may be proficient, equipped for every good work" (2 Timothy 3:17 NRSV).
—John Calvin: *The Proper Use of Scripture*

OCTOBER 9

## God's Promises

There are some big promises in Scripture. Here are two examples: "Those who seek the Lord lack no good thing" (Psalm 34:10). "Your night will become like the noonday" (Isaiah 58:10).

All the promises in the Bible are for you. An heir may ride over an estate and think, "This meadow, this cornfield, and this fine house are my inheritance." A stranger will not see these places with the same eye. In the same way, a secular person may read biblical promises and see them merely as stories. There will not be much personal interest in them. When a devout person reads the Scriptures and comes upon a promise, the proper response is, "This is part of my inheritance. It is mine and I am going to claim it."

—Jeremiah Burroughs
*Rare Jewel of Christian Contentment*

OCTOBER 10

## Spiritual Vitality

We will never understand prayer until we understand ourselves and the nature of God as revealed in

Scripture. If we do not regularly study the Bible, we will lack both the motivation to pray and the best guidance in how to pray. The dullness of our prayers is a result of our lack of familiarity with the Word of God.

It is not enough to read the Bible now and then. Our minds need to absorb its spirit. It is not enough to memorize facts about the Bible. Its teaching must touch our hearts. The Bible is food for spiritual growth.

—Hannah More: *Practical Piety*

OCTOBER 11

## *One Book*

I am a creature of a day, passing through life as an arrow through the air. I am a spirit come from God, and returning to God. Now I am hovering over a great gulf. Soon I will be gone and seen no more.

I want to know one thing. How do I arrive safely in heaven? God teaches me the way. He has written it down in a book. Oh, give me that book! At any price, give me the book of God.

I have it. Here is knowledge for me. Let me be a man of one book. I am far from the busy ways of others. I sit down alone. Only God is with me. In his presence I open, I read this book. Do I doubt the meaning of what I read? Is anything dark or intricate? I lift up my heart to the Father of lights. Lord, it is your Word. If anyone lacks wisdom let him ask God.

—John Wesley: *Works*

OCTOBER 12

## Interpretation of Scripture

"Many of the Samaritans from that town believed in Jesus because of the woman's testimony, which said, 'He told me everything I ever did'" (John 4:39). There is power in the authority of an individual's affirmation. Important issues depend upon it.

The Scriptures tell us what to believe regarding our salvation by Christ, but the authority of an interpreter is the key which opens the door to our understanding of Scripture.

—Richard Hooker: *The Laws of Ecclesiastical Polity*

OCTOBER 13

## Swear on the Bible

They asked me to take an oath. I said, "Ye have given me a book to swear on. The Son says in this book, 'Do not swear not at all' (Matthew 5:34). I obey the book and ye imprison me. Why don't you put the *book* in jail? How is it that the book is at liberty?"

As I was speaking, holding the open Bible in my hand, showing them the place where Christ forbids swearing, the judge said, "Nay, but we will imprison George Fox." The word got around that they gave me a book to swear on that commanded me not to swear at all, and that I was in prison for doing as the Bible said.

—George Fox: *Journal*

OCTOBER 14

## *Bible Promises*

My heart ached for my children who had been scattered throughout the wilderness by our captors. I was extremely fatigued and dizzy. Words will not express the affliction of my spirit. I opened my Bible and read this precious Scripture: "'Restrain your voice from weeping and your eyes from tears, for your work will be rewarded,' declares the LORD. 'They will return from the land of the enemy'" (Jeremiah 31:16). This was a sweet cordial to me when I was ready to faint.

My son, Joseph, arrived unexpectedly. He eagerly read from my Bible. "I will not die but live, and will proclaim what the LORD has done. The LORD has chastened me severely, but he has not given me over to death" (Psalm 118:17—18). He asked me to look at the comforting Scripture. "Have you read this?" I am writing this narrative for the same reason the Psalmist wrote. I am declaring the works of the Lord and his ability to keep us going, preserving us in the wilderness while held captive by an enemy. He promised to return us safely.

—Mary Rowlandson
*Narrative of Captivity and Restoration*


OCTOBER 15

## *Listening to Scripture*

We give the ability of spiritual awareness a variety of names. The old ones are probably best: "The hearing ear, the understanding heart." What is important is that the spiritual ear should be open to perceive and absorb, and the will to obey, what God speaks to even the dullest human heart, through the pages of the Bible.

This, and not logic, is the way to grow in religious knowledge. This is the way to know that the truths of religion are not shadows, but deep realities.

—John Shairp
*Hindrances to Spiritual Growth*

OCTOBER 16

## *A Queen and her Bible*

Religion is the ground on which all other matters take root. If the soil is corrupt, the tree will be sickly. I am a student of philosophy. Few professors have read more. I do not need to pretend that I am so simple that I do not understand it, or so forgetful that I don't remember any of it.

And yet, while reading many volumes, I have not neglected God's book. It gives us reason to believe (in a world where there is much wickedness and grief) that God would never have made us except for a better place and more comfort than we find here. No other creature lives in as much peril and danger as I do.

I see many who are overbold with God Almighty. They make too many subtle scannings of God's will.

They are like lawyers dealing with human testaments. Their presumption is so great, I will not accept it. I intend to guide them by God's holy rule.
—Elizabeth I: *On Religion, 1583*

OCTOBER 17
## *Living Word*
Scripture is the authority for the church. Human authority and wisdom are not the source of church doctrine. God is its source. St. Paul does not tell us that Moses was an excellent man or that Isaiah was very eloquent. He makes no effort to increase the credibility of the human authors of Scripture. He says they are instruments in God's hands. The Holy Spirit guided them. What they wrote is inspired. They are servants of the living God and faithful stewards of the treasures committed to them.
—John Calvin: *The Proper Use of Scripture*

OCTOBER 18
## *Understanding the Bible*
Difficult passages in the Bible are the product of our ignorance. Study it more carefully. Pay attention to more than the words. Ask who the original subjects and readers were. Consider the circumstances

surrounding the passage. Read it in context, noting what comes before and after. If you come across strange behavior or a cryptic statement, leave them with God. Let the scholars worry about them.

—Miles Coverdale
*A Prologue to the Bible*

OCTOBER 19

## Compare with Scripture

Inspired individuals wrote the Bible. God guided them. God's Spirit is consistent and cannot be supposed to be the author of any private revelations that are contradictory to the ones that sacred Scripture preserves for us. This would set the Spirit of Truth at variance with himself. If someone pretends that the Spirit has told them something, and Scripture does not confirm it, that person is simply mistaken. "Anyone who claims to be a prophet, or to have spiritual powers, must acknowledge that what I am writing to you is a command of the Lord. Anyone who does not recognize this is not to be recognized" (1 Corinthians 14:37f NRSV).

—Charles Chauncy
*Enthusiasm Described and Cautioned Against*

OCTOBER 20

## *One Book in Two Parts*

There never was and there never will be but one covenant of salvation between God and humanity. The substance of this covenant is Jesus Christ. Our Bible contains two Testaments or "Covenants". We have the authentic titles and contents of them, which we call "Holy Scripture" and the "Word of God." One we call *Old* and the other *New*. "'The time is coming,' declares the LORD, 'when I will make a new covenant'" (Jeremiah 31:31). The second is much better than the first. The first declared Jesus Christ, but from far off and hidden under shadows and images which vanished at His coming. "The time is coming and has now come when the true worshipers will worship the Father in spirit and truth" (John 4:23).

—Theodore Beza: *The Christian Faith*


OCTOBER 21

## *Light to the Blind*

I am amazed that anyone should speak against translating Scripture into every language of ordinary people. I can't believe that anyone would ever ask why it is necessary to give light to those who walk in darkness.

It has pleased God to send to England the Scripture in our mother tongue. No blind leader or false teacher can deceive you now. You may always know the true from the false.

—William Tyndale: *A Pathway into Holy Scripture*

OCTOBER 22

## *Old Testament*

When St. Paul speaks of Holy Scripture, he does not refer to the letters he was then writing. Neither did he have in mind the writings of other apostles and evangelists. His Scripture was the Old Testament.

It is clear that he valued the law and the prophets for the church of Christ. The law is not to be set aside and never spoken of again. We have no liberty to choose what we will. We are to respect the entire Bible. *All* Scripture is divinely inspired.

—John Calvin: *The Proper Use of Scripture*

OCTOBER 23

## *The Majesty of the Scriptures*

To be well informed is not everything. Some are thorough students of good doctrine, but completely lack enthusiasm and affection. Their acquaintance with God is little more than a fleeting fancy. Why? Because they have never understood the majesty of the Holy Scriptures. If we realized that God is speaking to us, we would certainly listen more attentively and with greater reverence. If we comprehended that while reading Scripture we are in the school of angels, we would be far more careful to practice what we learn in its pages.

—John Calvin
*Enduring Persecution for Christ*

OCTOBER 24
## *Search the Bible*
It is important that you read the book of the Lord your God. Let no day slip by without receiving some word from the mouth of God. Open your ears and he will speak pleasant things to your heart. Keep your eyes open. Let them see what is waiting for you in your Father's testament. Praise God's goodness and graciousness. In mercy, he has called you from darkness to light and from death to life.

—John Knox: *A Letter of Wholesome Counsel*

OCTOBER 25
## *Practical Scripture*
A great idea never took anyone to heaven. Religious opinion has little value. If it is false, it can be damaging. If it is correct, but not applied to life, it can intensify guilt. If it is inconsequential, it wastes thought that could be set on a higher level. Christ did not come to teach us this kind of religion. The Bible's teaching is sensible and useful. God did not give his Word, his

Son, and his Spirit to provide us with orthodox views and correct opinions.

—Hannah More: *Practical Piety*

OCTOBER 26

## *A Testimony*

George Fox said that Christ was the light of the world and that by this light all of us could be gathered to God. Impulsively, I stood up in my pew and wondered about his doctrine. I had never heard such before. He continued to open the Scriptures, saying, "The Scriptures were the prophets' words, and Christ's and the apostles' words. The Lord led them in their speaking. You will say, 'Christ says this and the apostles say that,' but what can *you* say? Are you a child of the light? Do you walk in the light? Is what you say given you inwardly from God?"

This opened me. It cut me to the heart. I saw clearly we were all wrong. So I sat down in my pew again and cried bitterly. I cried in my spirit to the Lord, "We are all thieves! We are all thieves! We have taken the Scriptures in words and know nothing of them in ourselves."

—Margaret Fell Fox: *The Journal of George Fox*

OCTOBER 27

## Understanding is Doing

"If I have the gift of prophecy and can fathom all mysteries and all knowledge . . . but have not love, I am nothing" (1 Corinthians 13:2). Paul calls the hidden, secret meaning beneath the prime significance of the Scripture a mystery. Knowledge is the understanding of practical things, such as Christian freedom, or the recognition that our conscience is not constrained. He is telling us that though we may understand the Bible in both its obvious and its hidden meaning, we may yet lack the important ingredient of love. The point is to use such knowledge to serve our neighbor. Otherwise, it is meaningless.

—Martin Luther: *Sermon on Christian Love*

OCTOBER 28

## Misinterpreting Scripture

Ministers of Darkness have made a mountain out of misunderstood verses of Scripture. Paul writes, "Women should remain silent in churches. They are not allowed to speak" (1 Corinthians 14:34). Read the entire fourteenth chapter to discover the context of that verse. The apostle is exhorting the Corinthians to love and to desire spiritual gifts. He urges them not to speak in an unknown tongue. He tells them to grow up and behave in an orderly manner. "God is not a

God of disorder but of peace" (1 Corinthians 14:33). It is only then that he says women should be silent.

It is clear that both women and men were disorderly. Paul instructs *men* to remain silent also. "If there is no interpreter, the speaker should keep quiet in the church" (1 Corinthians 14:28). The speakers he criticizes were not fully Christian. Paul does not place this limitation upon those who have the true message of the Lord Jesus. Men of this generation are blind when they quote such Scripture. They pervert the apostle's words and corrupt his original intention.

—Margaret Fell Fox: *Women Speaking*

OCTOBER 29

## *Fresh Translations*

Late this morning I read the story of Joseph and his brothers (Genesis 37—50). It melted my heart and drew tears from my eyes. The Sacred Writings tell the story simply and beautifully. It is a strange thing that the Bible is so little read. I am reading it regularly and plan to read it all. I dare say there are many people of distinction in London who know nothing about it. If some genteel bookseller were to publish the story of Joseph as an "Eastern Fragment," many would greatly admire it. They might even begin to place some value on God's Word. I have a great mind to make the experiment.

—James Boswell: *London Journal*

OCTOBER 30

## God's Truth

God has put his truth in the Scriptures. It is God's self-revelation. The Bible is seed that will not decay. "The faith and love that spring from the hope that is stored up for you in heaven . . . you have already heard about in the word of truth, the gospel that has come to you" (Colossians 1:5). St. John often speaks of the gospel as the truth, suggesting that without it we would know nothing. Scripture is the only solid foundation we have.

What difference would it make if we knew everything except God? If we don't know God, we are in misery. God has given us his Word. He presents himself to us in its pages. We can meet him there. He makes himself known to us. The Bible is our treasure. It contains the seed that will grow children of God. It is the nourishment of our souls.

—John Calvin: *Behavior in the Church*

OCTOBER 31

## All Valuable

Every part of the Scripture is valuable. There are genealogies and pedigrees, primitive instructions for dealing with lepers, and instructions on how to sacrifice goats and oxen. These passages seem to have little value for us today.

They may seem out-of-date and pointless, but God did not have them written for no purpose. There is not a sentence, not a clause, not a word that is not written for our instruction. Our understanding is the problem. There is nothing useless in the Bible. Scripture is like a pharmacy. All kinds of medicines are there. There is something for different kinds of diseases. Not every drug is for every illness. Those oxen and goats teach you to sacrifice the ugliness of your heart. You may have leprosy of your soul. Those genealogies lead us to the birth of our Savior Christ. Everything in the Bible is there for your good.

—John Jewell: *Of Holy Scriptures*

# NOVEMBER
## *Life in Christ*

NOVEMBER 1

## God's Respect

The world does not judge fairly. Tastes change, and it is partial to the current set of values. The world pays respect more by favor than by merit. Honor is an external thing. It exists only in the one who gives it. It is better to deserve respect and not have it, than to have it and not deserve it.

God respects you. That is the most important thing. You are a person of honor because you are God's child. "You are precious and honored in my sight, and . . . I love you" (Isaiah 43:4). Let the people of the world think what they will of you. God thinks well of you.

—Thomas Watson
*The Art of Divine Contentment*


NOVEMBER 2

## Beyond the Bible

I esteem the Holy Scriptures above all human treasure. Even more do I value the Word of God, which is living, potent, eternal, free, and independent of all elements of this world. It is God himself. It is Spirit and not letter. Because pen and paper are not involved, there is no way to erase or destroy it.

It is not possible for the Scriptures to make a bad heart good. But everything improves a good heart illumined with the light of God (a heart with a Divine spark in it).

—Hans Denck: *Writings*

NOVEMBER 3

## *The Risks of Prosperity*

Prosperity exposes us to the temptation of becoming "lovers of pleasure rather than lovers of God" (2 Timothy 3:4). The more luxurious the life, the more increased the danger. If we are young and lively, mingling in fashionable circles, we are on the brink of a hazardous precipice. The risk is that we may be drawn into a vortex of folly and indulgence that will destroy all sense of religion.

But Christian faith strengthens us against these temptations. They actually cease to be temptations at all. We can lose our taste for them. It is like growing up and ceasing to play with toys. Faith is the best preservative against the snares of prosperity.

—Hannah Sinclair: *A Letter to Catherine*

NOVEMBER 4

## *Like a Child*

Paul says, "When I became a man, I put childish ways behind me" (1 Corinthians 13:11). This is quite different from the little child which our Lord recommended for our example.

We should try, as we grow up and get to know the world, to have the simplicity of childhood kept fresh within us. If we allow the world to rob us of it, we may be sure that the world has nothing equal to give us instead. The only way to preserve this good thing, or to renew it, is to open the heart to simple, truthful communion with God and Christ.

—John Shairp: *Hindrances to Spiritual Growth*

NOVEMBER 5

## *How to Live*

These things will bring you quietness of mind. When you get up each morning, always commend yourself to God, asking him to defend both your soul and your body from the dangers of the day. Ask God to watch over your parents and friends, your teachers and your governors.

Take care of your business. Do not listen to gossip. Many will devise false tales. Give them no credit. Words are but wind, yet words can hurt. Let God shield you from uttering slander even against your enemy. Be gentle with everyone, even if they are not gentle with you. Keep God in mind. God says, "It is mine to avenge; I will repay" (Deuteronomy 32:35). You do not need to take care of it yourself.

—Isabella Whitney: *A Sweet Nosegay*

NOVEMBER 6

## Strength in Christ

Jesus Christ is the source of our inner strength. Many are not able to understand that we can receive strength from someone else. They think it is ridiculous to think that if we have a burden we can receive strength from outside ourselves. It would make sense to them if we had another person to come and stand under the burden with us. But it is a puzzle to think that someone else's strength can strengthen you, particularly when that person is clearly nowhere near.

A Christian receives strength through faith in Christ. Receiving Christ's strength in our soul enables us to do whatever God lays on us. Christ has the strength not only to save us, but also to support us in difficult times.

—Jeremiah Burroughs
*Rare Jewel of Christian Contentment*


NOVEMBER 7

## Genuine Education

Even as there is a difference in eating and cooking, it is one thing to hear and something else to learn. Two things keep us from learning—we do not recognize the value of the lesson and we forget what we hear or see. We are like sieves immersed in water that are full as long as they remain there, but quickly drain dry when removed. Jesus said, "Listen carefully to what I am about to tell you" (Luke 9:44). His teaching falls not only as dew that wets leaves, but also as rain which soaks to the tree's roots and makes it bear more fruit.

Perhaps you have heard a lot about Christ. But have you *learned* Christ? Learning Christ will make you like Christ. "And we, who with unveiled faces all reflect the Lord's glory, are being transformed into his likeness with ever-increasing glory, which comes from the Lord, who is the Spirit" (2 Corinthians 3:18). Anyone who takes a close look at Christ will be changed. A saint is a landscape painted by Jesus. To learn Christ is to live Christ.

—Thomas Watson: *The Art of Divine Contentment*

NOVEMBER 8

## God Will Take Care of You

God has offered to take us by the hand and lead us through the journey of life. The proof of the sincerity of this offer is in Jesus Christ. "This is love: not that we loved God, but that he loved us and sent his Son as an atoning sacrifice for our sins" (1 John 4:10). St. Paul triumphantly asks a question we can't answer. "He who did not spare his own Son, but gave him up for us all—how will he not also, along with him, graciously give us all things?" (Romans 8:32).

Trust God with undoubting confidence. Take God's hand with humble gratitude. Obey his voice. In sickness and in health, by night and by day, at home and in crowds, God will watch over you with inexpressible tenderness.

—Timothy Dwight: *The Sovereignty of God*

NOVEMBER 9

## *Enduring*

Our afflictions may be heavy, but they are not more than we can bear with the strength of Jesus Christ. If Christ could bear it, so can you. The Scripture assures us that the strength of Christ can be in us. "And we pray this in order that you may live a life worthy of the Lord and may please him in every way: bearing fruit in every good work, growing in the knowledge of God, being strengthened with all power according to his glorious might so that you may have great endurance and patience" (Colossians 1:10f).

When you are under any great hardship, live so that others may see such a Scripture made good in you.

—Jeremiah Burroughs
*Rare Jewel of Christian Contentment*

NOVEMBER 10

## *Cleanliness in a Dirty World*

"All who cleanse themselves . . . will become special utensils, dedicated and useful to the owner of the house, ready for every good work" (2 Timothy 2:21 NRSV). It is not easy to walk through mire and dirt without becoming dirty. If we go to a foul and filthy place, we will return with a stain or spot upon us.

Be careful in your association and conversation with anyone who despises God. When we are among bawdy and hypocritical people, we need to be careful in our conversation. Their behavior and attitudes easily infect us. We may have to live with them until we depart this world, but let's try to keep ourselves clean. Ask God to shield us from such filthiness, and to purify us by his Holy Spirit.

—John Calvin: *Vessels Unto Honor*

NOVEMBER 11

## *Inevitable Temptation*

Our Savior said, "Pray that you will not fall into temptation" (Luke 22:40). He did *not* say, "Pray that you will be spared temptation." It is important for us to be disturbed and tempted. God will be with us when these things happen. He will uphold and deliver us.

If you have been spared temptation, that does not mean you are a holy person. The most holy are the most tempted. The higher the mountain, the greater the wind.

—John Wycliffe: *The Poor Caitiff*

## NOVEMBER 12

## *Discipline*

I have seen the limits of worldly vanity. One moment I was in good health and had everything I could want. Another moment I was wounded and sick, having nothing but sorrow and affliction. Before I had experienced genuine affliction I sometimes thought I could wish for it. When I lived happily in prosperity, with all the comforts of the world around me and my family present, I would be bothered to think that I had not suffered enough. I envied others who were troubled by many trials and afflictions. I thought of the Scripture that says, "The Lord disciplines those he loves" (Hebrews 12:6).

Now the Lord has had an opportunity to discipline me. Some may receive their affliction one drop at a time. Mine came like a rushing flood. If I wanted to be tested, this captivity was an extreme testing.

I learned that when God asks someone to endure hardship, he is fully able to carry them through it. He is also able to show how the struggle has positive results. Like David, I can now say, "It was good for me to be afflicted" (Psalm 119:71). I have learned the emptiness of outward things. They are a bubble that bursts. They are shadowy vanities with no permanent value. God is our only hope.

—Mary Rowlandson
*Narrative of Captivity and Restoration*

NOVEMBER 13

## Working for Christ

There was once a monk who spoke to a distinguished man about the faith. He asked the man why he did not believe. His answer is instructive. "You yourself do not believe. If you believed, it would show in the things you do."

If you believe, where are your works? Your faith is something that is well known. Everyone knows that Christ was crucified. The whole world knows that his glory has not been spread by force and weapons, but by poor fishermen. The purer anything is, the better it functions. The Christian life purifies the heart, placing it very near the truth. The closer you examine it, the clearer the truth will become to you.

—Girolamo Savonarola: *The Ascension of Christ*

NOVEMBER 14

## Christian Conversation

Silence is wisdom where speaking is folly. Silence is always safe.

Some are so foolish as to interrupt and anticipate those who are speaking, instead of hearing and thinking before they answer. This is uncivil as well as silly. If you think twice before you speak once, you will speak twice as well. To speak pertinently, consider both *what* is fit, and *when* it is fit to speak.

In all debates, let truth be your aim; not victory. Try to gain, rather than expose, your antagonist.
—William Penn: *Some Fruits of Solitude*

NOVEMBER 15

## *Try it Yourself*

Coleridge said, "If you wish to be assured of the truth of Christianity, try living as a Christian." If you become a part of the process of renewal described by Scripture, your own experience of its truth (and the confident assurances of others) will be convincing evidence. This evidence will only satisfy you. It is of no value to an outsider. Such people will deny things they have not themselves experienced.
—John Shairp: *Hindrances to Spiritual Growth*

NOVEMBER 16

## *Ready for Harvest*

Take every opportunity you possibly can to lead others to Christ. Be a teacher. Demonstrate the glory they are missing. Lend them a hand. Convince them. Have nothing but the glory of God in mind. Do not do this to increase your self-esteem, or to enhance your reputation. You are not attempting to make disciples for yourself.

Jeering and scoffing, ranting and denunciation are not effective tools for reforming anyone. It should be

obvious that you only intend to help them. Be simple and plain. Choose the right opportunity. When soil is ready, the plough will penetrate it. Love, simplicity, and seriousness are always effective. Be patient. Fire does not always fly from the flint on the first stroke.
—Richard Baxter: *The Saints' Everlasting Rest*

NOVEMBER 17

## Pride

A proud and haughty spirit is dangerous. It is a barrier between you and God. "God opposes the proud but gives grace to the humble" (1 Peter 5:5; Proverbs 3:34). Are you puffed up with pride? Do you seek the praise of others? Do you want the highest honors? Are you angry when you are challenged? Do you enjoy celebrity? Do you defend your innocence rather than confess your fault? If so, you are a proud person. You are not likely to be familiar with God. You are your own idol. Even if you speak a few proper words, your heart will not understand what you are saying.
—Richard Baxter: *The Saints' Everlasting Rest*

NOVEMBER 18

## No Arm Twisting

Jesus Christ did not compel people to follow him. He persuasively taught essential religious truth and gave rules for moral guidance. He then left us to act freely, following the insight of an enlightened mind and a teachable temperament.

Our Savior clearly demonstrated the proof of his divine mission. He said he was the fulfillment of prophecy. He performed miracles. He invited people to think about what they were seeing and hearing and to evaluate him. "You know how to interpret the appearance of the earth and the sky. How is it that you don't know how to interpret this present time?" (Luke 12:56).

—Aaron Bancroft: *Sermons*

NOVEMBER 19

## Honest Intentions

Maybe you never intended to devote all your words and works, your business, studies and diversions to the glory of Christ. You never had a thought that whatever you do might be done in the name of the Lord Jesus, making them "a fragrant offering, an acceptable sacrifice, pleasing to God" (Philippians 4:18).

But suppose you had. Do good designs and good desires make a Christian? By no means. The road to hell is paved with good intentions. Here are the important questions. Is the love of God in you? Do you desire nothing but God? Are you happy in God? Is he your glory, your delight, your crown of rejoicing? "Whoever loves God must also love his brother" (1 John 4:21).

Is this commandment written on your heart? Do you then love your neighbor as yourself? Do you love everyone, even your enemies, even the enemies of God, as your own soul? As Christ loved you? Do you believe that Christ loves you and gave himself for you?
—John Wesley: *The Almost Christian*

NOVEMBER 20

## Basic Lesson

We are too ready to retaliate, rather than forgive. We fail to gain by love and information. We could hurt no one we believe loves us. Try, then, to see what love will do. For if others see we love them, we should soon find they will not harm us

Force may subdue, but love gains. If I get even with my enemy, the debt is paid. If I forgive my enemy, I oblige him forever.

Love is the hardest lesson in Christianity. For that reason, it should be the one we work hardest to learn. Difficult things are beautiful.
—William Penn: *Some Fruits of Solitude*

NOVEMBER 21

## The Futility of Moralizing

There is no way you will ever be able to alter the natural course of water by building dams. For a while you may stop the flow, but when the reservoir is full, it will either burst the dam or overflow it. It may run with more rage than it ever did before.

If you would alter the streams of your nature, attempting to run after the will of God, you will not be able to do it by damming it with instruction on what you ought to do. It does no lasting good to teach moral lessons about how to speak and think other than as we naturally do. For a little while we may stop the streams of our affections by teaching and other exercises. But these affections will weasel out now and then. Eventually, they will break down or overrun all of our dams and devices. "And the final condition . . . is worse than the first" (Matthew 12:45).

Any change must be made at the headwaters. Another watercourse will need to be dug for the rivers of our corrupt will and nature. Who can do this? The spring itself? No. God, and God alone, can accomplish it.

—John Bradford: *The Flesh and the Spirit*

NOVEMBER 22

## Sundays

Who bothers to read the Scripture? There are very few who bother. Everyone is preoccupied with personal business. There is one day a week reserved for religious instruction. We spend six days conducting business and then spend the day set aside for worship in play and pastime. Some wander in the fields while others go for a drink at a tavern. Is it any surprise that we do not know the rudiments of Christianity?

—John Calvin: *The Mystery of Godliness*

NOVEMBER 23

## *More than Rules*

Christianity is certainly the most perfect rule of life available, but it is far more than that. If we were innocent, a nice code of laws might have been enough. The law has no way of saving those who break the law. We would not find much comfort in examining the statutes that condemn us.

The gospel does not provide us with rules that preserve existing innocence. It gives the guilty a way to salvation. It is not designed to reach us in a state of purity, but in the urgency of sinfulness.

—Hannah More: *Practical Piety*

NOVEMBER 24

## *Following Christ through Persecution*

When we suffer for the cause of God, we are walking step by step after Christ. He is our guide. God does not demand of us that we pass through the world's insults and persecution, always ready to die if necessary. If that were the case we could object, declaring it a strange road. We are commanded to follow the Lord

Jesus. His leadership is too good and admirable to be refused. Jesus Christ walks before us as our Captain.

Are we so delicate as to be unwilling to endure? If we are members of Christ, we will be tried by many afflictions. These two things cannot be separated. The world considers suffering for the gospel to be a disgrace. We can see more clearly. "The apostles left the Sanhedrin, rejoicing because they had been counted worthy of suffering disgrace for the Name" (Acts 5:41).

—John Calvin: *Enduring Persecution for Christ*

NOVEMBER 25

## *Recognizable Behavior*

The one who is the most charitable and friendly is the most deceived. If you think well of everyone, believe everything they say and trust them to keep their word, you will be disappointed. But this kind of trust is a sign of open Christian love. Because of it, we are known to be servants of Christ.

If we love our neighbor, helping out in times of distress, if we are charitable, loving and friendly, then we shall be known to belong to Christ. If we do not care for our neighbor, or seek our own advantage with his damage, we will be rejected as unknown at the last day.

—Hugh Latimer: *On Christian Love*

NOVEMBER 26

## Fake Religion

Forced and artificial religion is heavy and lifeless. It resembles forcing a weight upward. It is cold and spiritless, like the uneasy submission of a wife married against her will. She is compliant toward a husband she does not love, out of some sense of virtue or honor. Adherents of fake religion give scant service to God. They do no more than is absolutely required. A law compels them and they will be reluctant to go beyond what it requires. They will interpret religious law to give themselves the most liberty from it.

The spirit of true religion is open and generous. The one who is completely dedicated to God will never think it is possible to do too much for him.

—Henry Scougal
*The Life of God in the Soul of Man*


NOVEMBER 27

## The Holiness of a Name

There is something more precious than gold, silver, and jewels. It is another's good name. Solomon says, "A good name is more desirable than great riches; to be esteemed is better than silver or gold" (Proverbs 22:1). You will take care of your own good name, as well as another's, if you give no false testimony. Never defame anyone with lies and slander.

Don't even think the worst about another person. You gain nothing by being suspicious and trying to interpret what someone has said or done. It is wrong to repeat gossip. If you tell evil tales and give untrue reports based upon suspicion, you are giving false testimony. God's commandment forbids us to speak any word that incorrectly harms another person. Even if it is the truth, it is sin if it is not spoken in love.
—Thomas Cranmer: *Catechismus*

NOVEMBER 28

## *Use of Gifts*

In First Corinthians Paul attempts to silence and humiliate self-aggrandizing Christians. The gospel provides a lot of knowledge of God and Christ. It delivers many wonderful gifts. He tell us some have the gift of speaking, some of teaching, some of Scripture exposition, others of ruling, etc. God gives great riches of spiritual knowledge and a treasury of spiritual gifts to Christians. Unfortunately, few use these gifts properly. Rarely do they humble themselves to serve others as love directs. Each person looks for honor and advantage, desiring to acquire advancement and superiority over others. Each seeks personal glory and wealth. Many seem to want to be recognized as the best Christian, outranking all others. Such persons pretend to deny themselves while they speak of love and faith, but they do not actually practice it. This is why fanatics and schismatics populate the world.

—Martin Luther: *Sermon on Christian Love*

NOVEMBER 29

## What God Requires

We are sent into this world to do our part. One may have a prominent part while another works in obscurity. Both are equally accountable to God. What is required of us is tailored to what has been given us. Our responsibility is in direct proportion to our ability.

—Hannah More: *Practical Piety*

NOVEMBER 30

## The Way

Life in Christ is not an enthusiast's dream or a visionary's reverie. It is not a replacement of responsibilities with fancy speculation that turns shadows into reality. It is an anticipation of eternal happiness. It is freely serving God and diligently trying to understand him. God's will is law and his word a delight. His Spirit is our guide. This happy expectancy belongs to all who sincerely love God and devote themselves to him, saying, "Let the light of your face shine upon us, O Lord" (Psalm 4:6)

—Hannah More: *Practical Piety*

# DECEMBER
*Signs and Symbols of Christian Life*

DECEMBER 1

## The Brevity of Life

"What is your life? You are a mist that appears for a little while and then vanishes" (James 4:14). Life is a turning wheel. The poets painted time with wings to show the swiftness of it. Job said, "My days are swifter than a runner; they fly away" (Job 9:25). Our life is but a day. Daybreak is infancy. The sunrise is youth. Full growth is midday. Old age is sunset. The evening is illness. The night of death soon follows.

How quickly this day is spent! Sometimes the sun goes down at noon and life ends before the evening of old age comes. Sometimes the sun of life sets soon after it dawns. Life is short.

—Thomas Watson: *The Art of Divine Contentment*


DECEMBER 2

## No Snobbery

No one can see everything. God has not given complete knowledge to anyone. One person has more understanding and an ability to express things better than another. The one who is able to do the best work should not put down the efforts of another. Ability is a gift from God. If you can see where a mistake is made, attempt to help fix it. Let your knowledge be mingled with love.

—Miles Coverdale: *A Prologue to the Bible*

DECEMBER 3

## *Envy*

Augustine calls envy the devil's sin. Satan envied Adam's glory and robe of innocence in the paradise of the Garden of Eden. If you envy the possessions of another person, you will never be satisfied with what God gives to you.

Envy stirs up strife. The envious person spends so much time worrying about the blessings someone else enjoys that he cannot appreciate his own blessings. This is self-torture. Cain envied his brother's favor with the LORD (Genesis 4:3–9). He soon began to think of murder.

Discontent upsets more than the person who feels it. It affects those who are nearby. This evil spirit troubles families, parishes, and entire communities. If there is only one string out of tune, it spoils all the music. One discontented spirit jars others with its discord. This is the bad attitude that breeds quarrels and lawsuits. "What causes fights and quarrels among you? Don't they come from your desires that battle within you? You want something but don't get it. You kill and covet, but you cannot have what you want" (James 4:1f).

—Thomas Watson
*The Art of Divine Contentment*

DECEMBER 4

## John's Baptism

Paul asked the Christians in Ephesus how they were baptized if they knew nothing of the Holy Spirit. "Then what baptism did you receive?" (Acts 19:3). It is a question we need to ask ourselves, that we may live up to our baptism. They told him they had received John's baptism. Some weak, well-meaning disciple of John's had ignorantly kept his name as the head of a faction. These are the ones who had complained to John about Jesus. "That man who was with you on the other side of the Jordan—the one you testified about—well, he is baptizing, and everyone is going to him" (John 3:26). These followers baptized here and there in John's name without directing the ones they baptized any further.

Paul explains to them the true meaning of John's baptism, how it actually pointed to Jesus Christ. As far as it went, it was good. "John's baptism was a baptism of repentance. He told the people to believe in the one coming after him, that is, in Jesus" (Acts 19:4). But it was not a stopping place. It was a beginning.

—Matthew Henry
*Commentary on the Whole Bible*

## DECEMBER 5

## *The Function of Sacraments*

The sacraments are valuable because they give public testimony of that grace which is already present in every individual. Baptism is administered in the presence of the church to individuals who already know Christ's promise. An adult is asked if he believes. If the answer is "yes," then baptism follows. Faith is present before the administration of the sacrament. Baptism does not confer faith. In the baptism of an infant, the parents acknowledge their faith. Since the child has been born into the household of faith, the child is regarded as a participant in the same divine promise as the rest of the church. In either case, the church publicly receives one who has previously been welcomed by grace.

—Ulrich Zwingli: *On True and False Religion*


## DECEMBER 6

## *The Value of the Sacraments*

The sacraments remind us that God is resident in the church. The house of God maintains his truth.

When we are baptized in the name of our Lord Jesus Christ, we are brought into God's household. It is the mark of our adoption. Because God is our Father, we are under his divine protection and governed by his Holy Spirit.

The Lord's Supper is a plain declaration that we are joined to God and made one with him. Our Lord Jesus Christ shows us that we are his body, that everyone is a member, and that he is the head that nourishes us with his substance and virtue. As the body is not separate from the head, so Jesus Christ shows us that his life is common with ours, and that we are partakers of all his benefits.

—John Calvin: *Behavior in the Church*

DECEMBER 7

## *Why Communion?*

Visible actions are not the primary part of Holy Communion. Each act has significance. It is the food of souls. As food, it will yield no nourishment without being eaten. We are to receive Christ and feed upon him as it were. We are to take him as our Lord and life, yield ourselves to him, and live in him. Christ "is your life" (Colossians 3:4).

The Lord's Supper keeps fresh in our minds what was done a long time ago. We are remembering a friend, the best of friends, the greatest act of kindness. And it is more than a recollection. It is also a celebration. We declare his death to be our life, the spring of all our comforts and hopes. Our participation in this sacrament tells the world that we are disciples of Christ.

—Matthew Henry
*Commentary on the Whole Bible*

DECEMBER 8

## *Provisions for the Journey*

Keep in mind that you are here only briefly. You have but a short way to go. Why do you need so many provisions for so brief a journey? A traveler only needs enough to sustain him to the end of the trip. We have but a day to live and it may already be the twelfth hour of the day. If God gives us enough to last until night, that is enough. Let us be content.

If you had only a brief lease on a house or farm, it would be folly to start building and planting. Why, then, do we pull down our souls to build up an estate? An immoderate thirst for the things of the world is spiritually destructive. If we have enough until sunset, we may be content.

—Thomas Watson
*The Art of Divine Contentment*


DECEMBER 9

## *Taking Communion Lightly*

"Whoever eats the bread or drinks the cup of the Lord in an unworthy manner will be guilty of sinning against the body and blood of the Lord" (1 Corinthians 11:27). Fearful believers should not be discouraged from participating in the sacrament by the sound of these words. This passage of Scripture is not intended to make serious Christians hesitate, though the devil has often taken advantage of it and robbed good Christians of their choicest comfort.

The Corinthians came to the Lord's Table as to a common feast. It was a banquet for them. They were more indecent at this sacred feast than they would have been at a social one. Paul told them to eat for hunger and pleasure at home, and not to change communion into a wild party. Holy things are to be used in a holy manner.

—Matthew Henry
*Commentary on the Whole Bible*


DECEMBER 10

## *Begin with Baptism*

The only way to be saved is through repentance and faith in Christ's blood. These are the inward baptism of our souls. The washing and the dipping of our bodies in the water is the outward sign. The plunging of the body under the water signifies that we repent and intend to fight against sin and lust with the help of God. Repentance and faith begin at our baptism, and continue unto the end of our lives. They grow as we grow in the Spirit. The more devoted we become, the greater is our repentance, and the stronger our faith.

—William Tyndale
*A Pathway into the Holy Scripture*

DECEMBER 11

## Stewardship

Prosperity brings a great responsibility. You must give an accounting for how you have used your resources. Are you rich in good works? You may be a private person, but you must answer to others. Do you contribute to charity? An estate is a loan. You are but a steward who manages it. Your Lord and Master will soon come along and demand, "Give an account of your management" (Luke 16:2).

The greater our estate, the greater our charge. The more our revenues, the more our reckonings.

—Thomas Watson
*The Art of Divine Contentment*


DECEMBER 12

## Symbols

Sacraments are reminders of Christ, a sign of something removed from us by time. "Do this in remembrance of me" (1 Corinthians 11:24). The sacraments are not objects of worship. They facilitate worship. We continue to break bread as Christ broke it in order to be reminded of what happened to his body.

—John Wycliffe
*Christ's Real Body Not in the Eucharist*

DECEMBER 13

## Influences

It is easier to catch an illness from someone else than to catch health. The bad corrupt the good more quickly than the good will convert the bad. Mix an equal quantity and proportion of sweet wine and sour vinegar. The vinegar will sour the wine, but the wine will not sweeten the vinegar.

Human sin is like a plague. It is an infection that spreads easily. When we pray the Lord's Prayer we ask God to "lead us not into temptation" (Matthew 6:13). Then we willingly expose ourselves to infectious evil.

—Thomas Watson: *The Art of Divine Contentment*


DECEMBER 14

## Eulogy for Luther

Good people have complained that Luther was too stormy and severe. I will not deny this. I agree with Erasmus: "Because of the magnitude of the disorders, God gave this age a violent physician." God spoke to Jeremiah: "Now I have put my words in your mouth. See, today I appoint you over nations and kingdoms to uproot and tear down, to destroy and overthrow, to build and to plant" (Jeremiah 1:9f).

I do not deny that the more ardent characters sometimes make mistakes. Human nature is weak and no one is without fault. But we may say of Luther as the ancients said of Hercules, "He is rough, but he is worthy of all praise."

Luther constantly defended purity of doctrine and kept a good conscience. He never mingled politics with church work. He had no interest in gaining personal authority or promoting his friends to high position. Such wisdom is not the product of human care. Such a brave and ardent soul as Luther's must be divinely guided.

—Philip Melanchthon
*Oration at Funeral of Martin Luther*

DECEMBER 15

## *Clothes*

Excess in clothing is a costly folly. The trimmings of a vain world would clothe the entire naked world.

Choose your clothes with your own eyes, not another's. The more plain and simple they are, the better. Let them be neither sloppy nor fantastic. Select them for use and decency rather than for pride. If you are clean and warm, it is enough.

—William Penn: *Some Fruits of Solitude*

DECEMBER 16

## *The Time of Times*

Our Lord knew he would suffer. The night of his arrest had arrived. He had spent the evening with his disciples, like a dying father in the midst of his family, mingling consolations and last instructions. He began a solemn prayer. "Father, the time has come" (John 17:1).

What time is it? The most critical time, a time more filled with great events than any time since time began. It is a time of atonement, of fulfillment, of concluding the old and introducing the new. It is a time of triumph, of creating a spiritual kingdom that will last forever. These are the events you commemorate in the sacrament of the Lord's Supper. Let it focus one bright point of light on everything that is important. Touched with contrition for past offenses, and filled with a grateful sense of divine goodness, let us come to the table with humble faith in his infinite mercy, and devote ourselves to his service.

—Hugh Blair: *The Hour and the Event of all Time*

DECEMBER 17

## *The Power of Satisfaction*

Patience and diligence, like faith, move mountains.

Never give out while there is hope, but do not have an unreasonable hope. That shows more desire than judgment.

It is wise to know when you have done enough. Do good with what you have, or it will do you no good.

Seek not to be rich, but happy. The first lies in moneybags, the other in a contentment which is not for sale. We put wrong labels on things. We call prosperity "happiness," and adversity "misery." Adversity is the school of wisdom and is often the way to eternal happiness. If you want to be happy, accept your condition and be indifferent about what is more than sufficient.

—William Penn: *Some Fruits of Solitude*

DECEMBER 18

## Confirmation

Heaven costs me nothing. It is a free gift. I am baptized and participate in the sacrament of the Lord's Supper. These confirm my assurance of heaven. I keep the bond safe and certain by living with respect for God and praying daily. When I have the seal of baptism and the Lord's Supper prefixed to God's promise, I am well taken care of.

—Martin Luther: *Table Talk*

DECEMBER 19

## Anger and Envy

Anger is less reasonable and more sincere than envy.

Anger breaks out abruptly. Envy is a preface.

Anger wants to be understood at once. Envy prefers remote ambiguities.

Anger dwells on an incident. Envy invents new ones at every repetition.

Anger tells a choppy, vehement tale. Envy's report is both smoother and more false.

Anger is imprudent and impatient. Envy is discreet—it has much to hide.

Anger does not delay. Envy waits for its best opportunity to hurt.

Anger soon runs out of breath. Envy has barbed arrows in reserve.

The angry person focuses on himself. The envious person focuses on the enemy.

Anger is a violent act. Envy is a constant habit.

Perhaps envy, like lying and ingratitude, is frequently practiced because there are no human laws against it. Determining the heinous nature of these sins that are above the reach of human punishment is reserved for the final justice of God.

—Hester Chapone: *Envy*

DECEMBER 20

## *Truth*

Nothing helps reason more than the coolness of those who offer it. Truth often suffers more by the heat of its defenders than from the arguments of those who oppose it.

When you are obligated to speak, be sure to speak the truth. Equivocation is half way to lying, and lying is the whole way to hell.

Believe nothing against another except on good authority. Do not report what may hurt another, unless it is a greater hurt to others to conceal it.

—William Penn: *Some Fruits of Solitude*


DECEMBER 21

## Cart before the Horse

Baptism is the very least of all the Christian requirements. It is a much greater commandment to love your enemies, to do good to those who do evil to you, to pray in spirit and in truth for those who persecute you, to subjugate the flesh, to discard pride, covetousness, impurity, hate, envy and intemperance, to serve your neighbor with everything at your disposal, to be free from every evil desire and unbecoming language, to love God with all your heart, and to bear the cross of the Lord Jesus Christ with a joyous heart. Can you compare baptism with any of these?

To baptize before a person has faith is placing the cart before the horse, to sow before plowing, to build before the lumber is at hand, or to seal a letter before writing it.

—Menno Simons: *Writings*

DECEMBER 22

## Paul's Great Discovery

"I have learned to be content whatever the circumstances" (Philippians 4:11). That text is a precious jewel that is small, but extremely valuable. Contentment is a hard lesson to learn.

Paul's ministry for Christ had put him into a great variety of conditions. "We are hard pressed on every side, but not crushed; perplexed, but not in despair; persecuted, but not abandoned; struck down, but not destroyed" (2 Corinthians 4:8). He demonstrates an indifference to his outward conditions. He gives us a map of his earthly route that leads to an incredible spiritual destination. "In troubles, hardships and distresses; in beatings, imprisonments and riots; in hard work, sleepless nights and hunger... through glory and dishonor, bad report and good report; genuine, yet regarded as impostors; known, yet regarded as unknown; dying, and yet we live on; beaten, and yet not killed; sorrowful, yet always rejoicing; poor, yet making many rich; having nothing, and yet possessing everything" (2 Corinthians 6:4-10).

Spiritual contentment is like a watch you carry in your pocket. Though it bounces around as you walk, there is no harm to its delicate gears and springs. It continues to keep perfect time. The things that happened to him did not damage the spring of Paul's heart. One experience did not lift him up only to allow another one to cast him down. The gears of his affections were not misaligned, but continued a constant motion toward heaven.

—Thomas Watson
*The Art of Divine Contentment*

DECEMBER 23

## *Promises*

Rarely promise. Avoid hasty resolutions also. Someone says, "I will never do this," and yet does it. "I am resolved to do this," says another, and yet has second thoughts about it, or does it awkwardly to keep his word, as though it is worse to break one's word than to make a mistake in keeping it.

Wear none of your own chains. Keep free while you are free.

—William Penn: *Some Fruits of Solitude*

DECEMBER 24

## *Christ Blesses Families*

Jesus Christ is the greatest blessing of the world. He is also a family blessing. By him salvation comes to a house. When we inventory family blessings, let's put Christ at the head of the list. He is the blessing of blessings. It is a great honor to be related to Christ.

—Matthew Henry
*Commentary on the Whole Bible*

DECEMBER 25

## *Another Child*

All of the world's wisdom is foolishness in comparison with Christ. There is nothing more wonderful than the unspeakable mystery of the Son of God, the image of the eternal Father, becoming fully human. He probably helped his supposed father, Joseph, in a carpenter's shop. When those who lived in Nazareth see him seated in divine majesty they will be astonished. They will say, "Lord, you helped build my house."

When Jesus was born he surely cried like other babies. His mother took care of him as other mothers take care of their children. He obeyed his parents when he was growing up. He helped them around the home. There were probably times when his mother, Mary, asked him, "Where have you been?"

If this simple, lowly, and ordinary beginning of the life of Christ does not offend you, wisdom and divine insight are yours. You have a special gift of God in the Holy Spirit. Never forget that our blessed Savior lived among us as one of us.

—Martin Luther: *Table Talk*

DECEMBER 26

## *God in Christ*

The greatest reason for calling Jesus the Son of God is because he possesses the spirit and perfection of God. Jesus is the only begotten Son because he is the perfect image and representative of God. He demonstrates God's love for the world. He yields himself sacrificially.

To know Jesus as the Son of God is not to understand what theologians have written about him or to figure out the mystical, incomprehensible union between Christ and his Father. It is something far higher and more instructive. It is to see God in Christ. It is to recognize his godlike purity and goodness. It is to understand his harmony with the Divine Mind. It is to notice the completeness of the love he gives to the purposes of God. To love Jesus as the Son of God is to love the spotless, loving purity of his soul.

—William Channing: *Love to Christ*

DECEMBER 27

## Cheerfulness

A contented spirit is a cheerful spirit. The Greeks call it *euthumeo,* a good spirit. Contentment is beyond patience. Patience is merely submission. Contentment is cheerful. There is nothing passive here. Rather than simply accepting a burden, the contented Christian takes up a cross. Paul says, "For Christ's sake, I delight in weaknesses, in insults, in hardships, in persecutions, in difficulties. For when I am weak, then I am strong" (2 Corinthians 12:10). He not only submits to God's dealings, he rejoices in them. He not only knows the Lord is just, he also knows the Lord is good.

—Thomas Watson: *The Art of Divine Contentment*

DECEMBER 28

## Sacrament

A sacrament is a sign of a sacred thing, of grace that has been given. It is a visible figure or form of the invisible grace, provided and bestowed by God's bounty. It is an analogy to something already done by God's Spirit. It is a public testimony.

—Ulrich Zwingli
*On True and False Religion*

DECEMBER 29

## New Wine

To say that all things new are bad is to say that all old things were bad when they began. Of all the old things ever seen or heard of, there is not one that was not once new. Whatever is now establishment was once innovation. The first inventor of pews and parish clerks was probably criticized in his day. Judges, juries, criers of the court are all the inventions of ardent spirits, who filled the world with alarm and were considered as the great precursors of ruin and dissolution. No inoculation, no turnpikes, no reading, no writing. The fool says in his heart and cries with his mouth, "I will have nothing new!"

—Sydney Smith
*Fallacies of Anti-Reformers*

DECEMBER 30

## Hypocrisy

It is amazing that the world should be offended by the one who raised the dead, gave sight to the blind, and hearing to the deaf. If they would consider such a person a devil, what kind of God would they have? But here it is. Christ would give the world the kingdom of heaven. They prefer the kingdom of earth. The highest wisdom and sanctity of the hypocrites sees nothing but secular honor, carnal desire, humdrum life, pleasant recreation, money and possessions—all of which will vanish.

—Martin Luther: *Table Talk*


DECEMBER 31

## The Church Extends Christ

The Church is greater upon earth than was Christ. I don't mean that the Church in itself is better and of higher rank than Christ. Christ is immeasurably better and higher and more precious than the Christian Church. But the Church covers a greater part of the earth than he walked. He did not travel very far. His public ministry lasted about three years. His Church endures for all time on earth.

—Martin Luther: *Sermon on Christian Love*

# BIOGRAPHICAL INFORMATION

JOHANN ARNDT (1555–1621). German Lutheran. Disturbed by disputes among the new Protestants. He wanted more emphasis on the spiritual life and less theological debate about the work of Christ. Produced four volumes of meditations and prayers.

AARON BANCROFT (1755–1839). American minister. Served as a Minuteman in the battles of Lexington and Bunker Hill. Attended Harvard. Began his ministry as a missionary to Yarmouth, Nova Scotia.

RICHARD BAXTER (1615–1691). British Puritan minister. Deeply involved in the political and social struggles of his day. Persecuted and imprisoned for his beliefs.

LYMAN BEECHER (1775–1863). American. Graduate of Yale who became an outstanding public speaker. President of Lane Theological Seminary in Ohio. Father of Henry Ward Beecher.

THEODORE BEZA (1519–1605). From Burgundy. Leading Huguenot theologian, and Calvin's successor as leader of the Swiss Reformation.

HUGH BLAIR (1718–1800). Scottish minister. Professor of rhetoric and *belles-lettres* at Edinburgh. Distinguished preacher.

JAMES BOSWELL (1740–1795). Scottish lawyer. Famous for his *Life of Samuel Johnson*. Widely traveled. His personal papers were recovered in the twentieth century.

JOHN BRADFORD (c. 1510–1535). British reformer. A prisoner in the Tower of London. Wrote extensively while incarcerated. Burned at the stake in Smithfield.

ANNE BRADSTREET, née Dudley (1612–1672). New England immigrant from Cambridge. Survival in the American wilderness was difficult. Expressing the faith that sustained her, she became America's first immigrant English poet.

MARTIN BUCER (1491–1551). German monk. He heard Martin Luther defend himself in Rome. Became a friend and supporter of Luther. Exiled to England. Queen Mary exhumed his remains and burned them.

JEREMIAH BURROUGHS (1599–1646). British minister. Member of Westminster Assembly of Divines. Prolific writer and popular speaker.

JOHN CALVIN (1509–1564). French. He embraced Protestantism while in college and concentrated on biblical studies. Calvin became the father of Presbyterianism through his community at Geneva, Switzerland.

THOMAS CHALMERS (1780–1847). Scottish. Ordained minister, but was also professor of mathematics and chemistry at St. Andrews. Ultimately, taught theology at Edinburgh and led formation of the Free Church of Scotland.

WILLIAM ELLERY CHANNING (1780–1842). American minister. Essayist at the heart of the literary and religious thought of his day.

WILLIAM HENRY CHANNING (1810–1884). Nephew of William Ellery Channing. Ordained after attending Harvard Divinity School. Eloquent preacher, transcendentalist, and social reformer.

HESTER CHAPONE, née Mulso (1727–1801). British. Self-educated aristocrat. Gained respect as a writer.

CHARLES CHAUNCY (1705–1787). Son of Boston merchant and grandson of Harvard's second president. Ordained minister. Influential liberal leader.

ANNE CLIFFORD (1590–1676). British. Countess of Dorset, Pembroke, and Montgomery. The only surviving child of George Clifford, Earl of Cumberland. Her handwritten diary records her struggle against laws that required male heirs.

MILES COVERDALE (1488–1569). Bishop of Exeter. Translated Bible into English. Contributed to the first *Book of Common Prayer*.

THOMAS CRANMER (1489–1556). Archbishop of Canterbury. Put English translations of the Bible in British churches. Was tried for treason, convicted of heresy, and burned at the stake.

HANS DENCK (1492–1527). Anabaptist from southern Germany. Excelled in ancient languages. Ascribed importance to "inner light" as a source of inspiration and guidance.

PHILIP DODDRIDGE (1702–1751). Born of Christian parents in London. Wrote enduring hymns, such as "O Happy Day," , "How Gentle God's Commands," "Father of Peace and God of Love," "Awake, My Soul, Stretch Every Nerve," "Great God, We Sing That Mighty Hand."

JOHN DONNE (1517–1631). English poet. An outstanding preacher in the Church of England.

TIMOTHY DWIGHT (1752–1817). American. Army chaplain during Revolutionary War. President of Yale. Lyman Beecher credited Dwight's preaching for his personal conversion.

JONATHAN EDWARDS (1703–1758). American pastor, theologian, and philosopher. Associated with both Yale and Princeton, he was one of the most influential thinkers of his time. His writings are strong expositions of Calvinism.

ZILPHA ELAW (born c.1790). American. Converted during a camp meeting. Active in black Methodist Church as an itinerant female evangelist.

ELIZABETH I (1533–1603). Daughter of Henry VIII. Queen of England 1558–1603. Elizabeth encouraged Protestantism in England.

NATHANAEL EMMONS (1745–1840). President of Massachusetts Missionary Society. Disputed with nearly every popular group of his day.

CHARLES FINNEY (1792–c.1850). Born in Connecticut, moved to rural New York. Religious conversion turned his studies from law to theology. An effective evangelist, he became president of Oberlin College.

GEORGE FOX (1624–1691). British shoemaker. Opposed state control of Church of England. Formed a Society of Friends (Quakers). Visited William Penn in America while traveling widely to preach.

JOHN FOX (1517–1587). British preacher, reformer, and writer.

MARGARET FELL FOX, née Askew (1614–1701). British. Married Thomas Fell (who became a judge and representative in parliament). Eleven years after her husband's death, she married George Fox, a frequent guest in their home at Swarthmoor. She became the nurturing mother of Quakerism.

EDWARD HART (dates unknown). Clerk of Court in Flushing, New York. Signed *Remonstrance of the Inhabitants of the Town of Flushing to Governor Stuyvesant, December 27, 1657.*

MATTHEW HENRY (1662–1714). British non-conformist minister. Noted for his huge *Commentary on the Whole Bible*, once considered to be the best commentary in English for devotional use.

RICHARD HOOKER (1553–1600). Leader in the Church of England. Preached at Oxford. Author of *The Laws of Ecclesiastical Polity* in which he refutes other Protestants as well as Roman Catholics.

THOMAS HOOKER (1586–1647). Immigrated from England to Holland and then to New England with John Cotton. Led a group of supporters from Cambridge to Hartford. An influential clergyman.

JOHN HOOPER (1495–1555). Bishop of Gloucester. Author of books on theology and church doctrine. Burned at the stake.

JOHN HOWE (1630–1705). British clergyman. Educated at Cambridge and Oxford. Puritan theologian. Chaplain to Oliver Cromwell.

# BIOGRAPHICAL INFORMATION ❧ 271

JOHN HUSS (1373–1415). From Czechoslovakia. Eagerly read Wycliffe while a student at the University of Prague. Eloquent spokesman for the Protestant Reformation in Bohemia, placing the authority of Scripture above tradition a century before Martin Luther.

ANNE HUTCHINSON née Marbury (died 1643). Banished from Massachusetts Bay Colony because of her criticism of Puritan clergy, she became one of the founders of Rhode Island.

JOHN JEWELL (1522–1571). Bishop of Salisbury. British reformer. Exiled under Queen Mary.

GEORGE JUNKIN (1790–1868). Ordained by the Associate Reformed Presbytery of Philadelphia. Defended Calvinism against its critics.

JOHN KNOX (c.1514–1572). Scottish reformer. A tough man for tough times. Befriended John Calvin in Geneva. One of the editors of the revision of the *Book of Common Prayer.* Final days in Edinburgh.

HUGH LATIMER (1485–1555). British reformer. Bishop of Worcester. Effective preacher who supported Martin Luther's ideas. Burned at the stake under Mary Queen of Scots.

WILLIAM LAW (1696–1761). English clergyman. One of the few Protestant mystical and devotional writers from the era.

JARENA LEE (born 1783). American. Active in Philadelphia's Bethel African Methodist Episcopal Church. Became an itinerant preacher in many states, speaking to both white and black audiences.

ROBERT LEIGHTON (1611–1684). Scottish. Studied at Edinburgh University and became its president. Archbishop of Glasgow.

MARTIN LUTHER (1483–1546). German leader of the Reformation who criticized the medieval church's abuses. Luther's theological position is that we are freely justified by God's grace and not by our good works.

PHILIP MELANCHTHON (1497–1560). Taught Greek at the University of Wittenberg. Close friend of Martin Luther. One of the gentlest spirits in the Reformation. Worked tirelessly for understanding and unity.

HANNAH MORE (1745–c.1833). British. Grew up in a scholarly atmosphere, learning many languages. Popular tract writer with international sales. Produced both sacred and secular literary works.

WILLIAM PENN (1644–1718). Founder of Pennsylvania. Son of an English Admiral. Expelled from Oxford.

Became a Quaker and imprisoned in London Tower. Sought refuge in America. Prolific writer.

ELIZABETH SINGER ROWE (1647–1737). First female English author of popular works. Isaac Watts published her religious work posthumously.

MARY ROWLANDSON, née White (c.1637–1710). Moved from England to Salem in 1639 and later married Joseph Rowlandson, a minister. A captive of Indians, she traveled with them from Lancaster, Pennsylvania, to New Hampshire. The account of her captivity is an early American classic, which can be read in *Boundless Faith: Early American Women's Captivity Narratives*, edited by Henry L. Carrigan, Jr., and published by Paraclete Press.

GIROLAMO SAVONAROLA (1452–1498). Italian Dominican. Anticipated Calvin's idea of a Christian commonwealth. Denied the authority of the Pope, trusting only his own conscience. He was hanged and burned.

HENRY SCOUGAL (1650–1678). British minister. Though an Episcopalian, he taught at King's College in Presbyterian Scotland where he is still considered to be among the great minds. He died early of tuberculosis.

FRIEDRICH SCHLEIERMACHER (1768–1834). German theolgian. Ordained in 1794 and preached in Berlin. Became a leading professor of theology. Worked for the union of Reformed and Lutheran Churches.

JOHN CAMPBELL SHAIRP (1819–1885). Scottish. Professor of Latin at St. Andrews and of Poetry at Oxford. Genial and loveable, he had many notable friends in the literary world.

MARY SIDNEY (1561–1621). Countess of Pembroke who worked closely with her brother, Sir Philip Sidney, and oversaw the posthumous publication of his works. Her poetic paraphrases of the Psalms are impressive.

HANNAH SINCLAIR (dates unknown). Scottish. Oldest daughter of Sir John Sinclair. Her personal writings were collected posthumously.

MENNO SIMONS (1496–1561). Dutch priest influenced by Luther, but had ideas that pushed reformed doctrine into uncharted territory. Many Dutch Anabaptists adopted his name and became known as Mennonites.

SYDNEY SMITH (1771–1845). English clergyman. Kindly, philanthropic and witty. He was a good preacher and had little regard for a mystical approach to faith.

ROBERT SOUTH (1638–1716). British minister. Held important positions at Westminster, Oxford, and Islip. Eloquent pulpiteer.

JEREMY TAYLOR (1613–1667). English bishop, theologian, and devotional writer. Objected to religious intolerance and the ruthless persecution of heretics.

Augustus Toplady (1740–1778). British minister. Converted by Methodists, became a Calvinist who debated theology with John Wesley. Wrote enduring hymns, including "Rock of Ages, Cleft for Me".

William Tyndale (c.1494–1536). British reformer. Translated New Testament into English against much opposition. Executed as a heretic.

Thomas Watson (d.1686). Puritan preacher and writer. Active in London's politics, he was imprisoned briefly with others who attempted to restore the monarchy. His manner of expression and illustration enlivens his communication of spiritual insight.

John Wesley (1703–1791). Son of a Church of England rector. Itinerant preacher who traveled widely on horseback. Organized and directed the popular Methodist movement.

Susanna Wesley (1669–1742). British. Mother of John and Charles Wesley as well as seventeen other children. Both her father and husband were ministers. She had to struggle with poverty and illness most of her life. Despite limited resources she took outstanding care of her family.

George Whitefield (1741–1770). British minister. Associate of John and Charles Wesley. Famous open-air preacher in England and American Colonies.

ISABELLA WHITNEY (born c.1550). British poet. Probably born to gentry in Cheshire. Became a domestic servant in London. Published two volumes of poetry.

ROGER WILLIAMS (c.1604–1684). Anglican priest. Emigrated to New England and taught in Salem and Plymouth churches. The Puritans considered his ideas offensive. He was to be deported to England, but escaped and eventually helped found Rhode Island.

JOHN WOOLMAN (1720–1772). Born in New Jersey, died in England. Child of Quaker parents and an enthusiastic member of the Society of Friends. His *Journal* is a classic volume of spirituality.

JOHN WYCLIFFE (c.1328–1384). British reformer. Made the first English translation of the Bible. In the introduction he wrote: "This Bible . . . shall make possible Government of people, by people, for people." Popular, but condemned as a heretic twice during his last four years.

ULRICH ZWINGLI (1484–1531). Swiss priest who agreed with Luther on the great issues of the Reformation, but disagreed with his interpretation of the Lord's Supper. Killed in a battle during Roman Catholic invasion of Zurich.